Elizabeth Turner has worked ⋯ finance industries. She is now ⋯ successful business that support⋯ ⋯⋯ ⋯⋯⋯⋯⋯ in their life (www.theblueskiesofautumn.com). Any profits from the book made by Elizabeth will be donated to the Red Cross.

Further praise for *The Blue Skies of Autumn*

'An utterly courageous, soul-shaking, unflinchingly honest account of what the event did to the author: of her descent into the Valley of the Shadow and, finally, her emergence from it. Readers will seldom encounter a more moving, ultimately inspiring personal Odyssey than this one'
Sunday Times

'One of the year's most moving books'
Daily Express

'A heart-felt story . . . of hope and optimism, healing and recovery'
Belfast Telegraph

'Her inspirational journey left me knowing that light does exist at the end of a dark tunnel'
Claire Nasir, *GMTV*

'Elizabeth Turner is remarkable. Rather than, very naturally, breaking under the grief and responsibility she was forced to carry, she decided to embrace life. Instead of sinking into despair, she chose joy, which is inspirational'
John McCarthy

'This is a story of great and powerful love – between a woman and a man, a husband and a wife, a child, and all those who, in the face of extreme tragedy, wrap their arms tightly around us and never let go'
Gill Hicks MBE

'The most amazingly moving, poignant and inspirational book. I was gripped from start to finish'
Sophie Kinsella

THE BLUE SKIES
OF AUTUMN

*A Journey from Loss to Life
and Finding a Way out of Grief*

Elizabeth Turner

SIMON &
SCHUSTER

London · New York · Sydney · Toronto

A CBS COMPANY

First published in Great Britain by Simon & Schuster UK Ltd, 2009
This edition published by Simon & Schuster UK Ltd, 2011
A CBS COMPANY

1 3 5 7 9 10 8 6 4 2

Simon & Schuster UK Ltd
1st Floor
222 Gray's Inn Road
London WC1X 8HB

www.simonandschuster.co.uk

Simon & Schuster Australia
Sydney

Photo p. 208 © Zoe Norfolk

A CIP catalogue record for this book is available
from the British Library.

ISBN: 978-0-85720-646-6

Printed and Bound in Great Britain by
CPI Cox & Wyman, Reading, Berkshire RG1 8EX

Dedicated to
my husband
Simon James Turner
and my son
William Simon Turner

Contents

Simon James Turner
17.7.62

Peace
It does not mean to be in a place
Where there is no noise, trouble or hard work
It means to be in the midst of those things
And still be calm in your heart
(Anonymous)

I stood on tip toe gazing into the distance
Interminably gazing at the road that had taken you . . .
We miss you
(Chi'in Chia's wife)

Elizabeth Turner, wife
William Turner, son
Born 14.11.01

Introduction

I had a list of things I wanted to do after Simon, my husband, died. It included spending as much time with our son, William, as I could; dealing with my grief so that I could move my life forward; and retraining so that I could work for myself. The last thing on the list was to write a book for William so that he understood the journey I had taken. The Chinese talk about life happening in seven-year cycles and so, seven years after 11 September 2001, this cycle of my life drew to a close. I finished writing the book just before my fortieth birthday.

Simon never made it to forty. He died two months after his thirty-ninth birthday. I often thought about him standing in the Windows on the World restaurant at the top of the World Trade Center, and always hoped that in the terrifying moments before he died he was able to look at his life and know it was the one he had truly wanted. But then, I wondered, would I honestly be able to look back at my own life on the day I died and know that I had lived it in the best possible way for me and William? After Simon died, being able to answer yes to this question became the benchmark for the rest of my life.

11 September 2001 was my Armageddon. On that day my

life stopped being what I thought it was. Everything I had been taught about the world from a young age felt like a lie – if you work hard, if you are good, if you are kind, everything will be fine. All the truths I lived by and everything I believed in were blown apart. I can still see it now, the tiny shards of my life exploding around me. How was I ever going to find all those pieces? Would I ever be able to pick them all up again? How could I piece them together, and even if I did how could I stick them back as a whole so that my life was strong and resilient once more? Would I always see the glue and feel the fractures?

I chose not to pick up the pieces immediately. Instead, I waited until all the tiny fragments of beliefs, dreams and plans fell quietly to the ground and I swept them up into a big pile. I stood back and looked at it and knew that from the shattered pieces I had to create something new. It sounds simple, but making that choice was the hardest thing I've ever done. I almost didn't make it. Today, the life that grew out of that decision has more colour, more depth, more people involved, more purpose, more love and more joy than the one I lived before. I am thankful for this every day and for all the choices I had and what lies in front of me now. I am even able to forgive the people who caused Simon's death because now I can honestly say that I appreciate my experience and the journey I made.

Today, if you ask me whether I'm living the best life I could, the answer is yes. Because Simon died and because I loved him so much, I faced many choices and through them found the framework for my new life. This book is a way of explaining to my son who his mum is, and of reintroducing myself to friends in the only way that seems right. It's a way of showing others who have to deal with grief that there are many ways to handle it and that ultimately their choice will be the right one. There is no quick-fix solution. My story may help people or it may not, but I believe it can offer hope that there is a way through the worst experiences if you are able to 'quiet the mind and move deep within the soul' (Neale Donald Walsch).

PART I
FACING

Chapter One

I woke up on my own on Tuesday 11 September 2001. It was a beautiful autumn day with a bright blue sky, sunshine and a riot of colours that cascaded over the road. It was as perfect as it could be. I looked at my tummy. It felt huge and I gently rubbed it. I had enjoyed my pregnancy and didn't even mind my big stomach as it held a baby and I was pleased by how easy and healthy it had all been. Even though I was seven months pregnant and would have preferred to spend the day in bed I had to get into work at Channel 4 Television that morning where I was the Senior HR Manager. I had one more month before I was due to go on maternity leave but there was a lot to organize before I could leave my job to everyone else. I felt very peaceful and happy with my place in the world.

I rolled over and grabbed my mobile from the bedside table. My husband, Simon, was away on a business trip and I always liked to know that his plane had landed safely. I listened to the message. Of course he was OK. He was always OK. I don't know why I needed so much reassurance from him whenever he travelled, but he was pretty good at dealing with his hormonal wife. He was the kindest man. He phoned when I asked him to and reassured me even when I didn't know I needed it. I smiled as I recalled him asking, 'Can you tell me when you're being hormonal?' I laughed. 'If I knew I'd tell myself!' I pressed the button on my phone and deleted the message telling me that all was well.

I thought back over the last few days. The previous weekend had been a nesting one, dealing with impending baby issues. We had been to the Royal Free Hospital to look around the maternity ward, and had chosen essential baby equipment in John Lewis. It was so much fun even though I felt big, fat and tired. Simon, being the perfectionist he was, in both design and practical terms, took on the responsibility of examining all the equipment. We looked at cots, cot beds, bed linen, monitors, buggies, prams, sterilizers, bottles . . . the list was endless. But even we as excited parents drew the line at the Winnie-the-Pooh-themed baby manicure set. We couldn't help laughing. How had we ever become old and responsible enough to bring another life into the world? Neither of us was sure we should be allowed to do this; but if we kept quiet and looked competent in front of the staff, perhaps they might not report us!

That Sunday night I sat on the sofa watching *The Sopranos*. The baby was kicking and I watched Simon wandering around the house getting everything ready for his trip to New York the next day. He sat down and I stretched my legs across his. We talked about our lovely weekend and Simon repeated his favourite phrase, 'It's just so great being us.' It was. I looked at him and from the bottom of my heart and in my most serious voice, said, 'I love you.'

'Is that a real "I love you" or a get-out-of-jail one?' he asked.

'A real one!' I laughed. 'I can't believe how wonderful our

life is and what a happy weekend we've had together. I'm so happy that I'm about to have my first child and it's with you, and I love you so much. Thank you for being with me and making me feel so safe and loved.'

He leant over and kissed me and for a split second we knew that this was a moment we'd both remember as true.

'I love you too, wifey, and that's not a get-out-of-jail one either.'

It was Monday morning and once again I was lying in bed. I liked to leave it to the very last moment before I got up and left for work. Being pregnant, the more quality time I spent in bed the better I was at my HR job. As I lay there I watched Simon getting ready. He put on his purple shirt, his cufflinks and cream chinos, slapped on some aftershave and gathered together all the things he'd need for his trip. I smiled at the military precision with which Simon folded and packed all his clothes. He used to be a Sergeant Major of the Honourable Artillery Company in the City of London and had been part of the Armed Services for nearly twenty years. His ability to iron a shirt and fold clothes into something the size of a stamp was one of the things that made me love him more and terrified me all at the same time. Nothing had changed that morning, and as I watched him I thought how handsome he looked.

I was tired from all the things we'd done but finally managed to pull myself out of bed and off we went to the tube station.

I left Simon buying his ticket because I was late. A quick kiss and I dashed up the stairs to the platform as only a waddling pregnant woman can and a strange thought rushed through my mind: 'If anything happens to Simon I won't have had this last tube journey with him.'

Simon's destination, New York, was a big part of our life. He worked there and we both travelled there regularly together. He was the Publishing Director of the Risk Waters Group, a London company specializing in financial and technological publications, and he had to go on business trips to America once a month. When he was there he worked out of the company's offices in SoHo with views downtown of the Twin Towers, and occasionally the company held conferences in the Windows on the World restaurant on the 106th floor of the World Trade Center. On 10 September 2001, Simon flew to New York as the representative of the directors to host a conference. He did mention where the conference was to be but I hadn't paid a huge amount of attention.

Once again I enjoyed the beauty of the day on my way to work. I could smell the beginning of autumn in the air, and the blue of the sky was so spectacular that I noticed it more than once that day. It was such a vivid deep blue that you could see for miles and it lifted the spirits. It hinted of wonderful things. I suddenly felt a 'what a fabulous life this is' moment. I was pregnant, I loved my husband deeply and everything was perfect.

I arrived at work and it was a busy but relaxed morning. People came in and out of my office talking to me and I enjoyed my chilled frame of mind. This was an unusual state to be in because Channel 4 was a dynamic but hectic place to work. However, Simon and I had just come back from a holiday in Dorset. We had decided that we should have a last holiday on our own together before I went on maternity leave in October.

I was still holding onto the wonderful feeling you create on holiday before it disappeared into a dream again.

We had our weekly HR management meeting arranged for the afternoon so Jane Jordan, my colleague, suggested we have lunch beforehand. It was midday UK time and just as I was collecting my things to go for lunch my phone rang. We had been married for two years and I still felt excited when I knew it was Simon on the phone. He had showered and was ready to leave to go to the World Trade Center for his conference.

'Did you get into work on time?' he asked.

'Very funny,' I replied. 'Anyway, I need to talk to you about the Mamas and Papas buggy we want. I phoned John Lewis and it's not in stock and I've looked on the internet and I can't find anywhere that sells it.' Even I could sense the feeling of irrational panic in myself.

'Look, wifey, we'll have the buggy in time for when Spot arrives,' said Simon.

Simon had nicknamed our baby Spot after a conversation with a colleague. 'Congratulations, what are you hoping for?' his friend asked and Simon quickly replied, 'I want a Dalmatian puppy but Elizabeth has her heart set on a baby.' Even I thought that was one of Simon's funnier jokes and so Spot was christened.

On the subject of the buggy, Simon managed to calm me down as always. 'When I get home,' he sighed, 'I'll sort everything out and now you need to stop worrying.'

He calmed me down. He made me laugh. And yet at the same time I always felt that he took care of me, protected me and kept me secure. This was no mean feat for any man as I had a scary independent streak which for some reason made me feel that I had to face the world on my own all the time. Simon even got to the point where he gently reminded me, 'As I'm your husband now, Elizabeth, it's absolutely fine for you to accept money from me!' And I had been happy to relinquish some of my independence because I respected and trusted his integrity so much.

We chatted some more. I loved the feeling I had when I connected with him. I was so at home with him and felt so lucky that of all the people in the world I had found my way to him. It was more than I had ever wished for.

The rest of that conversation will forever be private to Simon and me. I felt a sense of loss when I put the phone down, as I hated it when we were separated. The end of the call felt funny. I looked at the phone. Should I call him back? We had said all the little things that showed each other what we felt and we'd had a lovely call so why did I need to phone him again?

At about 1.45 p.m. UK time, Jane and I returned after our lunch. I walked into my office with its own television and saw a news flash on Sky News. A plane had hit the World Trade Center in New York. I couldn't take in that information. One minute I was sitting in the Channel 4 café downstairs with Jane and Ian Dobb, the Head of the IT department; the next I was walking up the stairs and, with every step and each tick of the clock, I came closer to a massive change in my life.

I saw the TV screen sitting on my desk holding the image of the Twin Towers with smoke billowing out of one of them, and the 'Breaking News' tag line. I looked at it all and tried to absorb what it was telling me. A cold shiver of panic rippled through me, but as soon as it came it disappeared. It left an impact, though. I felt that my soul knew something and it was trying to tell me but I didn't understand its language. Very quickly my logical mind jumped in and told me all the statistics, facts, figures, numbers and calculations that prove bad things are rare happenings. I didn't want to listen to my intuition as I was scared it could be telling me the truth. I knew Simon was in the Twin Towers, although I didn't know where, but I reminded myself that I lived a normal life, I was pregnant, and that everything would be fine. Of course I would be all right and so would Simon. We were about to have our first child and fathers don't die just before a new baby is born. I stopped listening to my soul – my inner knowledge – and protected myself.

Jane walked into my office.

'Have you seen the news, Elizabeth? This is unbelievable!'

'I know,' I replied. 'Simon is in New York in the World Trade Center.'

I didn't look at her face in case she could see the fear that was reflected in mine. We both turned back to the screen. There was a small black mark on the left-hand side which the TV camera was following. It flew very close to the buildings. The reporters were frantic as they shouted that it was another plane. They sounded like radio commentators when a footballer was close to scoring a goal. They spoke urgently, faster, their voices reaching a crescendo. I followed the small mark and felt everything move into slow motion. We watched as it flew right into the second tower. No goal had been scored. Something horrific had happened right in front of our eyes. The small black mark just disappeared into the side of the building and erupted into a gigantic fireball. Two planes had slammed into the World Trade Center. You could almost feel the world stand still, frozen in utter disbelief. Then the energy shifted and in that moment the world became a different place.

I looked at Jane and we stared at each other.

'It has to be an attack of some sort,' she said, eventually. Our rational brains tried to make sense of something that looked completely irrational. I didn't know what to do or think – should I panic, cry, scream or stay calm? I just stood there. I was frozen to the spot but could feel the adrenalin begin to pump through me. Fear! Fight or flight? What do you do when you don't even know what you are fearful of? What do you do when you feel in the pit of your stomach that everything beautiful in your life may have just ended?

I stood motionless in my office and tried to work out what was going on and what to do. At a cellular level I knew Simon was about to die and I wanted to scream, but instead I pushed instinct away and clung only to the facts.

I decided to phone his mobile but got no answer. That was not unusual as the reception in the World Trade Center was bad and there had been previous trips when I couldn't get hold of him when he was there. There weren't enough facts to panic properly about yet. So I decided to phone Simon's office in New York, and when I couldn't get through I rang Risk Waters in London.

'Everything is OK. We've spoken to David Rivers [Editorial Director of *Waters Magazine* in New York] on his mobile – he sounded calm and they think a bomb has gone off but they're all OK and they're being evacuated.'

'It's not a bomb,' I said. 'The Twin Towers have been hit by two planes and the buildings are on fire.'

'Honestly, we've heard from them. They said that it was getting smoky on the 106th floor and they were being moved to the floor above. They've been told that they're being evacuated and that everyone is OK,' the receptionist said.

Through the floor-to-ceiling glass of my office I could see everyone watching the images on the banks of TVs all over the channel, hanging from the ceilings, on people's desks, in people's offices. Word was getting round that Simon was in the World Trade Center. I knew people were starting to look at me and like a scared animal I retreated to a safe place. I closed the blinds on the glass and switched off the television. I sat in my chair and looked at Jane. All of our HR experience was useless in this situation. I was so used to working with manuals and procedures and codes of conduct that my instinct was to reach for something to tell me what to do. But there was no manual for this.

My boss Peter came in and he, Jane and I tried, very rationally, to work out what to do, as good Human Resources people do in a crisis. We always held a management meeting on Tuesday afternoons so I said, 'I think the best thing to do is to carry on with it. If Simon's going to phone he'll ring my mobile.' I sat in the meeting going through all the normal points we had to discuss and all the time I kept thinking, 'This will not happen to me,' and 'If I don't allow myself to think anything awful can happen then it won't.' I felt that if I willed Simon to be alive then that was what would happen.

The afternoon limped on as I waited to hear from him. People came and went from their offices, watched the screens and carried on with their day. I was trying to phone Simon again when Jane came in and told me very calmly, 'Elizabeth, the buildings have both collapsed.' At precisely that moment my phone rang and it was my sister, Catherine. At last, I knew I could let go. Relief rushed through my body as the brave exterior fell away. My family knew who I was. I wasn't a London career woman with a big job and a big title. I was their little sister who was desperate for help. I collapsed crying on the phone to her.

Catherine was also heavily pregnant.

'Please don't tell me Simon's in one of the towers,' she demanded.

'He is! I can't get hold of him and nobody has heard from anyone at the conference for ages now.' I was close to hysterical.

'Ron and I are coming to get you,' Catherine decided.

I sat in my office with Jane and tried to compose myself. I didn't want to go down and meet Catherine and her husband Ron while crying – I didn't want people staring at me.

I was standing in the foyer of Channel 4. All the TV screens were behind me but I wouldn't look at them. The business of the day went on around me but life as I knew it had changed completely. I felt that if I allowed myself to let go of my normal world I would never come back to it. I could almost hear the protective barriers hurtling to the ground, locking down for good. I didn't know how long it would be before I unlocked them and stepped back out into the world – I didn't know if I ever would.

Catherine and Ron arrived to drive me home. It was nearly 6.00 p.m. and from that moment my world moved into slow motion and became dreamlike. I can recall some moments very clearly and yet there seemed to be a misty fog around much of what happened.

The car pulled up outside my house and Helen, my neighbour, came straight out to meet us.

'Elizabeth, I saw Simon with his suitcase yesterday. Is he in New York?'

'He is, and I can't get hold of him.' I was already on autopilot as I walked past her and into the house.

Andy Pringle, my other neighbour, came down the stairs. On Sunday Simon and I had invited him over to look at the small box room which we had decided to use for the baby. I'd had a big panic about the room smelling of paint when the baby was born, so we'd asked to have it painted now. Simon, of course, knew how best to deal with my disproportionate fears and got Andy over quicker than the speed of light. He'd started painting the room that day. Now he looked at me.

'He's in the World Trade Center, isn't he?'

'Yes,' I replied quietly.

Much of the rest of the evening involved Ron force-feeding Catherine and me with takeaway pizza to keep our energy up. News reports filled every channel of the television, and everyone was talking about what they had seen. Ron knew, by this stage, that Simon was involved in a hugely significant event. Even if he had survived the buildings' collapse he was still part of something traumatic. He phoned a few of the people from Risk Waters again to see if they had any more information, but all the connections in New York had gone down as the communication mast was on top of the north tower of the World Trade Center. There were no calls going into the city and none coming out. Tony Gibson, one of the directors who worked with Simon, repeated that they had heard from David Rivers after the first plane hit that they were being evacuated. They had been on the phone all day to members of staff, speakers, exhibitors and delegates from the conference. They were able to establish that there had been sixteen members of Risk Waters staff inside the building and that instead of the hundred and fifty delegates only sixty-five had actually arrived. Any further information was very difficult to find. They regularly received garbled third-hand messages saying that everyone had been evacuated safely only to discover that the authors of the messages hadn't been at the conference. The lack of information was frustrating.

I don't remember any of the evening at home. It was the end of the day and I didn't really understand what had just happened to my life. I knew that the planes had hit the buildings and I knew that the buildings had collapsed and that I'd had no contact with Simon. I decided to believe that Simon had been taken to a hospital and that he could have concussion and didn't know who or where he was. I needed to be loyal and to make sure I didn't give up on him until I definitely knew what had happened. If I didn't believe he was still alive, what hope did he have? What if he was trapped in the rubble, praying for me to get help? What if he was relying on me and I gave up on the first night? I had to trust that he was alive and that he was coming home to me and our unborn baby. I decided my determination, trust and resolve would bring Simon back safe and sound.

I got into bed and listened to his answer machine message over and over again to hear his voice. Where was he? Find me, Simon. Call me. Come home. That night I started talking – to the sky, to the ether – I didn't know who or what, I just pleaded. My father was a vicar and I had always prayed with Mum and Dad at night. We said thank you for our day and everything we loved. It was a special ritual but I didn't really understand why we did it. For some reason that night I didn't want to say I was talking to God. I didn't know if anyone was listening but that ritual somehow felt more important than it ever had before.

Chapter Two

It was early August and I was six months pregnant with William. Simon and I were both asleep in the dead hours of morning just before the alarm went off. All of a sudden, Simon sat bolt upright, shaking and crying, his face imprinted with fear. I woke up immediately and asked him what was wrong.

'I dreamt I was working in New York and I died. I knew I'd died and I couldn't get back to you and the baby. It was like I was stuck behind a glass window and I could see you but you couldn't hear or see me and it didn't matter what I tried, I couldn't touch you both,' he repeated.

I pulled him close and held him. 'It was just a dream. We're both all right. Perhaps it's a feeling of fear because you're about to become a father?' I suggested.

Simon's dream did scare us both but I don't believe we admitted that to each other. The thing that made it worse for me, however, was a dream I'd had a year earlier. I was just about to start my job at Channel 4, and since Simon was on a work trip to New York I decided to join him for a week. I was going to spend a few days shopping while Simon worked, then we'd booked a long weekend in the Hamptons for Valentine's Day, staying in a beautiful old hotel; we were really excited about spending time together.

When we arrived at our hotel in New York quite late in the afternoon we went straight to our favourite restaurant. We were newly married and everything was on an upward curve. I was about to start a glamorous new job, Simon had just taken over as a director for Risk Waters and we were very relaxed and happy.

That night we went to bed and that was when it all started to feel wrong. I had a dream that was so vivid I felt as though I was right inside it. It really frightened me. I was walking on my own through the streets of New York on a beautiful day. Manhattan's grey skyscrapers reached up into the sky where the glass and steel contrasted sharply with the deep, clear blue. I could see the windows at the top of the buildings, clearly defined and glinting in the bright sunlight. Everything was peaceful and still and I felt the calmness I'd enjoyed that afternoon with Simon before we went to bed.

A small white bird flew into view. I watched it fly until I realized it wasn't a bird but a plane travelling silently across the sky. As I watched, the plane exploded. Now I could see the blue sky, the grey skyscrapers and the orange ball of flames from the explosion. Everything remained silent and I watched the debris falling through the sky like matches until there was only a line of smoke. I felt sick and terrified and a hot fear rose from my stomach. I gasped for breath and felt overwhelmed with dread, but at the same time I didn't understand why I was so scared. I was on the ground and I was fine.

I woke up and it was morning, with Simon fast asleep beside me. Everything was normal. But what made this dream different was that it stayed with me, intense and vivid, for the rest of the trip and for a while afterwards. Instead of enjoying my first day in New York, going shopping and visiting galleries, I was holed up in bookshop after bookshop, frantically trying to read up on dreams and discover what it all meant. I developed a deep fear of flying from that day and the horror I'd felt coloured my view of everything that happened while we were in New York.

On the same trip I asked Simon if we could go to the Windows on the World restaurant together. I'd been up there once before on a previous trip but for some reason I really wanted to go again, and I badgered Simon about it. He finished work one night and I met him at a bar in SoHo where he introduced me to one of his colleagues and asked if I'd like to go to dinner with them. I wanted to go to the World Trade Center and knew that we couldn't do it any other time so I got cross and Simon and I had a big row about it. He'd been so many times before that he didn't want to do it again and I couldn't believe how selfish he was being. So we argued all the way to the Twin Towers about our differences of opinion. When we arrived Simon ushered me through the bag checks, gates and lifts. I stood in the foyer and looked at all the glass, marble, shiny chrome and crystal chandeliers. It was very 1970s and despite the enormous scale of the building it felt rather dated.

Simon and I got into the lift with everybody else and we all stood close together without speaking. I knew I was in a bad mood from the argument we'd had but aside from this I felt a deep unease, which I was at a loss to explain, slowly beginning to build. I'm not scared of heights or lifts, and I don't get claustrophobic, but I really didn't like the World Trade Center.

When we got there I thought the bar and restaurant were beautiful – luxurious and dynamic. I had a strong sense of the deals that must have been done, the power lunches, the rich and influential of Manhattan, all there within those walls. Simon went to get me a drink and I stood by the floor-to-ceiling windows looking out over the Manhattan evening. The sun was dipping down through a grey dusk and the people and traffic of New York moved below me like a colony of ants. Everything was too small and I felt as though I were in a separate space to the rest of the world. An unsettling thought came into my mind that if anything happened to the buildings, like a fire, nobody inside stood a chance of getting out. The feeling of fear and dread I'd had after my dream returned and I actually felt tears prick my eyes at the thought of it happening.

Simon came over with our drinks.

'Are you all right?' he asked me.

I looked at him. 'I hate being here. I don't like the building suddenly and I want to go.'

Simon was understandably pretty cross at this point, as I'd been so adamant that I wanted to come here, but we finished our drinks, went back to the elevators and stood in the small box as it plummeted back through the centre of the huge concrete building. I hated all of it – the windows, the height, the lifts, and the laughter around me when all I could see was confinement. We got to the bottom and walked out into the square. I drew a huge breath of fresh air and we walked away. I didn't look back.

Alone in my bedroom on the night the towers collapsed, even in the midst of my torment there was something that niggled at the back of my mind. It kept coming back however many times I tried to push it away.

I remembered the dreams and what I'd felt that evening at the World Trade Center. Unsure whether I was losing my mind altogether, I wondered whether they had been some kind of sickening prophecy or warning.

I didn't know much about synchronicity but I knew something felt odd. It was a feeling of recognition. Somewhere deep inside there was something irrefutably familiar about what had happened: I had known that Simon was going to die.

Chapter Three

My eyes opened in the morning. It was Mum and Dad's wedding anniversary, 12 September 2001. But instead of celebrating their day and hoping for my marriage to last for forty-five years I was praying it wasn't over after only two. I had a split second of normal life before my nightmare crashed back down on me.

I quickly rolled over, just like the morning before, reached for my mobile phone and dialled Simon's number.

'Please answer, please answer, please answer,' I whispered, but the call went straight to his answer machine. I ached for a message like the previous morning, but today I was living a different life. Everything had changed and the fear I'd held back from the previous day gripped me tight. He should have called by now. I slowly repeated pressing the numbers and got the answer machine again. I wondered whether Simon was still unconscious in a hospital somewhere, or asleep in the hotel and didn't hear my call, or couldn't find a phone that worked or was trapped under the rubble and waiting for someone to find him. I hoped one of these was true.

Catherine came and lay on the bed next to me while I phoned Simon's hotel to see if he had gone back there the previous night. I had to start eliminating the mad list of things I was compiling in my head that might explain what had happened to him. Simon had stayed at the Pickwick Arms hotel. It wasn't flash, posh or expensive but he liked it. Maybe if he was a regular and they were fond of him they would help me.

The hotel receptionist answered the phone and I asked to speak to Simon. He made an internal call and told me that no one was answering the phone in that room. I asked if he might send someone up to see if Simon was there. I wondered how many hotels in New York were being asked to check rooms for anxious relatives. The receptionist came back and told me that there was no one in his room. I put the phone down and looked at Catherine. 'He's not there but I know he's not dead. This sort of thing doesn't happen to someone who's seven months pregnant,' I declared as convincingly as possible. It was as much for me as it was for her. I was almost daring her to tell me that she thought he was dead already but she simply nodded her head.

The reality of the day returned as Deborah and Mark, my other sister and brother, arrived at the house from their homes in the North of England. It was a Wednesday in the middle of September and most of my family are teachers. They should have been with their classes in the middle of the day. But now nothing about life was as it should have been.

Everything started happening around me. People were finding places to sleep, others were cooking in the kitchen, the phone rang and there were lots of conversations going on. I could see all this activity but was cocooned in silence. I felt like I'd been put into another room with a glass window to look through. All I could hear were my emotions and thoughts. Screaming. Crying. Fear. Terror. Questions. 'Where is Simon?' 'I am pregnant.' 'What am I going to do?' 'I can't manage this.' The thoughts wouldn't stop or go away. I didn't know how to switch them off. I craved silence when I looked at the world around me, but couldn't get rid of the noise in my brain. It was going to drive me insane.

The house filled up with friends and everyone was sitting around having cups of tea and coffee. It really is true that everyone drinks tea in a crisis! One of my friends, Sarah, got up to leave and I went into the hall with her to say goodbye and to give her a hug. I opened the door and as I looked out into my drive I saw two men and a woman standing there in suits with briefcases.

'Can I talk to Mrs Turner, please?' asked one of the suited men.

'That's me,' I replied. 'Who are you?'

'We're from the *Daily Express* and we'd like to ask you to comment on the death of your husband in the World Trade Center.'

I was vaguely aware of the enormity of what had happened, but my focus was on Simon's absence and not the rest of the world. Suddenly I was being introduced to all the other implications that came with my new situation. I staggered back into the hallway and hid behind the door as Sarah explained that I didn't want to talk to the press. I was completely stunned. I didn't know what to do. Sarah closed the door and Ron rushed through to ask what had happened.

'The press are out there!' I screamed. I felt sick with shock. 'The *Daily Express* wants to ask me about Simon being dead!' I could barely stand up. Ron opened the door and politely asked them to leave and waited until they had gone.

We all decided at that point that I couldn't open my own door again or answer my phone until the press interest died down, although when that might happen was unclear. In less than twenty-four hours I had become public property and I don't think any of us had been prepared for that.

I felt horribly vulnerable. Simon and I had done a lot of work to our house but we were nowhere near the point of choosing curtains and putting them up and as the living room had large Edwardian sash windows it was like a cinema screen to the outside world. Eventually a friend tacked up lengths of voile so the press could no longer see inside.

I had never experienced anything like it. On the one hand I was disgusted and yet on the other I struggled with the thought that if I talked to them maybe they could help me find Simon. If his photograph was plastered all over the papers perhaps someone would find him. I felt helpless not knowing the right thing to do. One of the other families from Simon's company had decided to talk to the press about their daughter and when I read their story and saw the pictures I panicked and began to play the addictive yet futile game of 'what if'. What if they find her and I don't talk to the papers and then I don't find Simon? What if I don't go down the most obvious route? The media can sometimes elevate a person's situation and things happen because of the extra publicity. What if the Americans are only concentrating on their own people and I need to raise the profile of the British people that are missing? What if Simon is trapped in rubble and I don't get our press to print his picture?

I played this game a lot and it only served to scare me and panic me even more. I couldn't help myself. When people told me what a silly and useless game 'what if' was, I still quietly played it, but didn't tell them what I was coming up with. Then I felt guilty that I was still playing the game.

Catherine and Ron decided they had to leave that evening to go back home and get clothes and make arrangements for staying with me in the longer term. They had been there from the start and it was a huge loss when they left. I knew they were coming back but I really needed them both around me. Yet on another level I felt jealous that Catherine could go back to her home while I had no choice but to stay in the nightmare. I couldn't say that I didn't want to do it any more, or step out of the experience even for a moment. I felt that all my choices had gone.

My bedroom became my sanctuary. I walked in that night exhausted. My friend Jane Perks, who had introduced me to Simon, suggested that it might help if I wrote my thoughts down, so I found an old notebook to use as a journal. I couldn't switch them off or turn the volume down so I tried to write them out of my head. I wrote about my struggle over the press, about my panic, my terror, my shock and just the sheer absence of Simon.

I was so used to being in control of my life – my career, my life in London, my future – but this was all too big for me to handle. I didn't know how to deal with it and knew for sure that I was out of my depth. I also realized that nobody else knew how to handle it either. Nobody had any idea what was right. There simply wasn't a book of instructions and instead it felt as though we were feeling our way in the dark. I think that was why I began to talk at night to whatever I hoped was out there. I was desperate to talk to someone who knew what to do, but even at that point I sensed that talking to myself would only make everyone think I had really lost the plot. So I waited until I was alone in bed and talked to the night. I didn't know what I was doing or if it would help but I didn't think it could do any harm and who was to say that someone wouldn't answer? I decided to call whatever it was The Universe.

I sat cross-legged on my bed.

'Help me. Whoever or whatever is up there, I've never really asked for help before. OK, I know sometimes I've asked for a new bike or to pass my exams. I'm sorry for that, but I really need help now. I'm terrified. I can't live my life without Simon. I'm having a baby and I can't do that without him. Please help me! Send me anything that will help me!'

On and on, I continued in this vein. I really don't know what I expected to happen, but at least it felt like I was doing something. I have never asked for anything in my life with so much intent. I knew this request was coming from my very core.

Friends and family came in and out. Conversations were held all over the house with me and without me. Food was churned out and cups of tea were made but the situation didn't change. Simon didn't ring and he didn't arrive home. Every hour we were slowly moving further and further away from the time it had happened, and his lack of contact scared me more and more.

On Thursday 13 September, I met DC Amanda Urand for the first time. She was the Family Liaison Officer assigned to me and my family by the Metropolitan Police. She would act as a go-between for me and any other police department involved in the investigation, allowing me to get used to one person as a point of contact rather than having to talk to many different people. She had phoned the day before to introduce herself but didn't realize until she met me that I was seven months pregnant. The family liked Amanda straight away. She was efficient and organized, yet warm and compassionate, and she shared our irreverent sense of humour, which in this situation was proving to be an essential quality.

She arrived that first time with another liaison officer to support her. Mark and I sat in the lounge with them while Amanda sensitively explained the mountains of forms I needed to fill out to help them post Simon as missing and identify him when he was found.

'He's going to be fine,' I told her firmly. 'He was in the Territorial Army, so he knows how to deal with situations like this.'

Amanda nodded her head. She knew it wasn't her place to say anything until they had clear information to the contrary. Her male colleague provided us with information from the Foreign and Commonwealth Office.

'They're in the process of organizing flights for the families who are involved in the attacks.'

'Oh great,' said Mark. 'Is there any chance we could get the first flight they have to the Maldives?'

Mark, Amanda and I burst out laughing, but the other liaison officer sat looking stony faced. Amanda quickly understood the dynamics of my family and decided it would be best if she came on her own in future to support us.

Then she looked at me and quietly asked if I could describe Simon to her.

*   *   *

Over Christmas 1996, I came out of a long-term relationship and for the first time found it hard to deal with my new single status. My mum used to tell me how she met Dad. She had been engaged but at the last moment broke it off because she didn't feel her fiancé was truly the love of her life. Within eighteen months she had met and married my father and knew she'd found her lasting love. Because of this, I believed that when you met the right person you would really know. But I was twenty-eight and had begun to fear I might be chasing an unrealistic dream. I bought a flat and decorated it. I worked hard on my career. I travelled all over the country training retail staff on how to develop themselves personally and how to be assertive, and all the while I wasn't sure whether what I was saying actually worked. It wasn't working for me.

At the time I was working at Wallis, the UK womenswear company, and my boss, Jane, was also a very good friend. Henry, her husband, had invited his best friend to supper one Friday evening and she asked me to join them. The men had a tradition of cooking each other a meal for their birthdays and it was Simon's turn to cook for Henry. Jane explained the routine: they cooked together, talked, drank good wine and got very drunk. Jane had just had their first child, and frankly needed some company since she couldn't join in.

I'd had a very busy week travelling around the country, and although a quiet evening alone with a glass of wine and an episode of *Friends* doesn't rank up there as the most exciting thing to have planned, I was really looking forward to it. I ummed and ahhed for ages but in the end decided to go and help Jane out.

That was the night I met Simon, and realized you do just

know when you've met the right person. Jane and Henry went off to bed and left Simon and me talking on their patio until four o'clock in the morning. We had so much in common and seemed to agree on everything we were talking about. He was in the Territorial Army and halfway through the conversation he looked at me and said, 'You do know I do this, so there'll be times I have to be away quite a lot.' I couldn't believe he was already looking into our future.

It was only our third date when I knew I would marry him. My previous relationship had been with a lovely man. I could easily have married him and had a very nice life but there was something vital that wasn't there. When I met Simon I thought, 'That's it, that's what's missing.' I didn't know what 'it' was, but I knew I'd found it in him and it was right for me.

We met in August 1997 and the following August went on holiday to Italy. We had a standing joke that I wanted to be married by the time I was thirty and while we were away I had my thirtieth birthday. He was planning to take me to a special local restaurant but I was ill and spent the whole day in bed.

I didn't know whether Simon would propose that holiday, but I knew in my heart that it was a case of when, not if, and we were so happy together that I wasn't worried about it at all. He still managed to completely surprise me. On a warm summer's night in Tuscany Simon presented me with an engagement ring he'd designed himself in New York. It was exquisite. I was so overwhelmed by the ring that I forgot to reply.

'What's your answer?' he asked fearfully.

'Absolutely!' I gasped. 'It's just that the ring is a huge responsibility.' We both laughed.

35

We had met and married within eighteen months. It was all very fast but I was thirty and he was thirty-six and we both acknowledged that we'd done a lot in our lives and knew we should be together. The wedding was important to us but the most significant part was standing up and saying we were committing to being together for the rest of our lives. I would have gone anywhere and done anything with Simon. He came before my family where no one else ever had. He was the most important thing in my life and to be able to say that was an amazing feeling. We both had a sense of, 'That's it, we've found it. How lucky is that?'

It's easy to wax lyrical about our relationship, but it's worth adding that Simon was a perfectionist, unbelievably anal, had a very irritating temper, and spent far too much time working out our present and future life on spreadsheets. I was strong-

willed, independent and focused, but needed to be liked by everyone. Sometimes the stress of maintaining this appearance was unleashed when I came home. I would collapse with tearful exhaustion and Simon took the brunt of it. It's important to keep a balanced view of our amazing life: we were normal.

My mum used to say that I needed someone who would challenge me all the time and Simon did that, intellectually and emotionally. I didn't want to change anything about him. Even the parts of him that irritated me were things that made Simon the man I loved. On Valentine's Day 2001 I told him not to buy flowers as it was such a silly commercial thing. We laughed about all the fools spending their money and later that day I got a call from reception saying flowers had been delivered. They were from Simon. He said I wasn't expecting it so that's why he did it.

He had huge integrity and respect for other people. He was always kind and people used to tell me wonderful stories about the little things he'd done for others. Celine was probably Simon's best female friend and they worked together as directors at Risk Waters. She was from Dublin and had all the warmth, care, love and honesty that only the Irish can bring. On her birthday she came into work to find that Simon had left glasses of champagne and smoked salmon and blinis on her desk.

From a career point of view Simon was driven but I never felt it took over his life. He was very ambitious but he saw his friends and finished work early enough for us to go out to dinner and have weekends together. One male friend told me that Simon was the one who held all their friendships together. He remembered birthdays and anniversaries and kept everyone in touch.

Simon made me laugh a huge amount, as we shared the same sense of humour. He loved telling stories and was able to relate anecdotes in such a way that people could really visualize the image. He also embellished the stories in order to make them funnier and richer and everyone accepted and loved the fact that he did this. At the summer wedding of my friend Jill, all the guests were asked to talk to the man filming the wedding video and share their thoughts about the day. Everyone took it in turn to wish Jill and Steve love and happiness for their future together, and then the camera focused on Simon.

'My wife and I were walking through the grounds of this beautiful house when we came across these lovely people having a wedding. I have absolutely no idea who they are but the food has been delicious, they've chosen the finest wines and we've had simply the best day. Thank you whoever you are.' Nobody else wanted to be filmed after that.

We still had tiffs over who'd emptied the dishwasher last and all those 'living together' problems, but we really didn't argue that much. We both had a huge appreciation for each other.

We pooled our resources and moved into our dream family home at the end of 2000. The house was in a real state and we set about gutting and renovating it. I'd just had my thirty-second birthday and was concerned that if we were going to start a family we should think about it sooner rather than later. The house might be in a state but it could take several years to conceive.

Two months later on a quiet Saturday morning Simon was sitting at the table reading his paper when I leant over and showed him the blue mark.

'What's that?' he asked.

'It's telling us we're going to be parents!'

We were delighted, but standing there in the bombsite of a house we realized the enormity of the task we'd just set ourselves. Every single night and weekend we stripped paint, cleaned floors and did DIY around workmen who were rewiring the house and putting in new heating systems and damp proofing. When I was six months pregnant I wire-wooled the old parquet floor on all fours, trying to revive it so that we didn't have to put down a new floor. It was such hard work but it was all ours. We lived upstairs for nine months and only moved back down in July 2001 when family came to visit over the summer holidays.

Even then it all felt perfect. I had fallen pregnant so quickly and it was obviously meant to happen that way. Simon was really excited about it. Like most prospective parents we were apprehensive because we had no idea how a baby would affect our life. But it did feel as though this was where we were naturally heading. I remember he used to say, 'Will you marry me? Oh yes, we've already done that!'

While I was describing Simon to Amanda, I began to recall more and more memories about him and particularly remembered two trips we'd taken for his thirty-eighth and thirty-ninth birthdays. In July 2000 we went on a tour of the D-Day landing sites in Normandy – Juno, Gold, Omaha and Utah beaches. It was an area that Simon was fascinated by. I naively thought that because he was in the TA he was simply interested in the facts and figures of an army going to war and how that was done. Just before we left we saw the film *Saving Private*

Ryan and silently watched the opening scene with its graphic and realistic portrayal of guns, ammunition and death. It was horrific.

I turned to Simon. 'Do you ever truly think about the reality of what you're involved in?' He looked at me.

'What do you mean?' he asked.

'You're in the army and could be called up at any time if world events suddenly changed. You'd be asked to kill people in the name of your country and you could be shot or killed yourself.'

'I know,' Simon said, 'but you accept that when you sign up for the army. It's part of the job and that comes with every-thing including the great friends and social events.' I knew he meant what he said but I also knew that the reality of being called up was different.

In Normandy we stood on the beaches and in the museums and it was moving to see where the D-Day landings had taken place and the effect the event had had on history. We enjoyed the poignancy of our trip but in true Simon style our holiday also involved lots of dinners out, drinking French wine and wandering around Honfleur. It was a lovely time together.

In 2001 we decided to go away again to celebrate Simon's thirty-ninth birthday and he said that he'd like to visit the Somme region. I couldn't believe we were going to a war site again, but I remembered that our Normandy trip had been fun and relaxing and I knew that was what we needed. I was five months pregnant and we had spent the whole of my pregnancy renovating the house. We were desperately in need of a break from DIY and workmen.

Our trip began with a lovely drive through England and France to our destination. We drove from cemetery to cemetery looking at the white gravestones of thousands of young men who had died in the First World War. We saw the enormous monument at Thiepval with thousands of names etched onto it. But the most moving moment was our visit to the Beaumont-Hamel region and the Newfoundland Memorial. You can see the fields where the Battle of the Somme took place and the outlines of the trenches where the soldiers engaged in battle. The energy of the place was vivid. We had a tour guide and Simon walked with him listening to all his facts and stories. I walked with them but didn't listen. I looked at the deep holes cut through the fields like arteries across a body. The trenches were covered in grass and the area was almost peaceful. But you could feel the sadness and the fear of young men and their hopes and dreams being soaked in blood.

It sounds dramatic but I had a powerful sense of the feeling in that area. The tour guide told us that more than 19,000 young men had died in those fields on the first day of the Battle of the Somme. They knew that once their time came to move to the front trenches the likelihood was they weren't coming back. They were there because everyone who had gone before them had already gone over the top and been killed.

Each tour we took revealed more death. Name after name after name of men killed in their youth. There were lists on memorials, lists on headstones, lists on wall plaques. Everywhere we drove there was a cemetery, a cross or a battle site. The graves were so beautifully kept and so peaceful. I walked up row after row of immaculate white crosses and gravestones. Some had names and regiments beautifully etched across the front and others were marked with the words 'Unknown Soldier'. A body but no name.

I was curious about this trip now. 'Why are you so fascinated by Normandy and the Somme?' I asked Simon. I don't think he'd truly answered this question before, even to himself.

'I look at the graves and the trenches and the beaches,' he said, 'and I wonder what it would feel like to stare death in the face. What comes over you – is it fear, courage or some sense of knowing? I think deep down I want to know what it would be like and how much courage these men must have had to do what they did. I won't know in this lifetime because we're essentially living in a time of peace. But because of that, I think I need to know how other people have done it.'

There was a huge part of him that wanted to know whether *he* would have had the courage to go over the top in the Somme. Would he have been able to jump off the boat at the Normandy beaches and run to shore in a hail of bullets?

I thought this was a very honest answer and found the conversation helped me understand Simon more. As we drove away from the Somme we passed one last cemetery and decided to stop and have a final walk around before we left. I felt very emotional and could feel the sadness in my throat as we wandered among all the young men's graves. I rubbed my tummy and thought how lucky our baby was going to be to be born in Muswell Hill with nothing like this around. Suddenly, Simon shouted and beckoned me over to one particular grave. I looked down at the beautiful chiselled writing. There was the name of a soldier, and his regiment. The Honourable Artillery Company. The same army unit that Simon was a member of in the TA.

*　　*　　*

That night in my bedroom I wrote and wrote about what I was feeling and thinking. The dreams, the visit to New York, and the birthday trips felt important in a way I couldn't adequately explain. Had they been a warning? I started to wonder whether these coincidental experiences weren't such a coincidence after all.

What struck me as extraordinary was that Simon had been so fascinated by war and courage and what his own response might have been if he'd had to face death. He believed it couldn't happen to him. Yet although we lived in a time of peace Simon had faced a terrible death and one that would have required huge courage from him. I couldn't help wondering about the significance of it all, and the impact it was having on me now. Where previously the dreams, the trip to New York and our holidays had been subtle events that you might chat about over a dinner party, they now felt like messages with sledgehammer proportions. Were Simon and I being prepared for events we couldn't have imagined at the time? Once again I couldn't escape the feeling that this was familiar to me. Even I knew it sounded odd, but my intuition was beginning to feel stronger than my rational mind.

I remembered the poignancy of the Unknown Soldier – the body without a name. Now I had a name but no body.

Chapter Four

The first bunch of flowers arrived. I hated them.

'This isn't a morgue. I don't even know that Simon is dead yet!' I screamed, until someone took them away. Every morning the volume of post grew. Deborah and Catherine dreaded it. 'Only an hour before the post arrives,' I heard Catherine remind Deborah one day as they prepared themselves for the onslaught. We all sat in the lounge and listened as the postman pushed more and more envelopes through the door. We used to count how many pushes he made each day. I appreciated the fact that everyone was thinking about me and the baby and was deeply touched by all their kind words. On the other hand, I didn't want to be in this horrific situation. I sat on the sofa every day and stared at the vast pile of envelopes. I wondered what the postman thought was going on. Some of them had postmarks from the White House, Buckingham Palace, New York, Downing Street and the Foreign Office. It made no sense to me.

The mornings were always the worst part of the day. I woke up to a reality which left me feeling sick and in a vile temper, which Deborah and Catherine had to deal with. They lovingly put up with my anger and my hysterical sobbing, and all the difficult decisions that had to be made. I ricocheted between the fear that Simon might be dead and the hope that came from there still being no body.

I dealt with this dilemma by refusing to accept that Simon was dead until it was officially confirmed. As in a film, there would be a knock at the door and a solemn-faced police team would ask if they could come in and then I would be told the fact that the person I loved most in the world had been killed. It was my right to collapse at that point. But so far, no one had knocked on my door or given me the prompt to collapse. I didn't want to have to deal with that thought until everyone else agreed to play along with the script. The longer I ignored the truth the better. I would hold onto the hope that Simon was alive and was coming home to me and the baby, until someone had the common courtesy to tell me officially that he was dead.

Ron, Deborah, Catherine and Mark had other worries. They were concerned about the impact of the stress and trauma on me and the baby and decided that I should go to the maternity ward Simon and I had already visited. This proved fruitless, however, as none of the midwives knew me and nobody wanted to provide advice or guidance. Deborah was left to plead with my GP to do a home visit, which under normal circumstances was very much outside his remit. Eventually he was persuaded to come and after taking my blood pressure and listening to the baby, it seemed that everything was all right. Everyone was reassured.

I was the only person in the UK who was pregnant by someone caught up in the event, which intensified the press interest in my situation. I could see the reporters from my bedroom window sitting in their cars outside. I watched as they systematically went around my neighbours asking if anyone would be willing to talk. I later heard that they had found my old flat and pestered the new owners who didn't know Simon or me very well at all. They found my father's old church which he had retired from in 2000 and asked the new vicar where Mum and Dad lived and if they could see our wedding certificate in the church records. They found my parents in the home they had retired to in Yorkshire, and Catherine who lives on a remote farm down a dirt track in Northamptonshire. I was very shocked by the lengths the press went to to find their story.

Three days after 11 September there was a knock at the door and Ron answered it.

'Excuse me for disturbing you,' said a rather young, pregnant journalist from the *Sunday Times*. 'Can I talk to Mrs Turner? I have some idea of what she must be going through as I'm pregnant too.'

'With all due respect,' replied Ron, 'if you truly knew how she felt, you wouldn't be here at all.' Ron shut the door.

This journalist wasn't prepared to take no for an answer and went down the street knocking on my neighbours' doors and asking questions. Ron asked her to leave again.

'I appreciate you have a job to do,' he told her, 'but please can you go and do it somewhere else. What you're doing is very intrusive and upsetting for someone who already has more than enough to deal with.'

Finally Amanda went out and presented her warrant card.

'Good morning. I am DC Amanda Urand. If you continue with this course of action I will have to arrest you for harassment,' she said calmly.

The journalist eventually left but it wasn't the end of the

press interest. The first picture of Simon appeared in the *Daily Mail* on Friday 14 September. Mark and Ron had walked up to the shops to buy some essential provisions and collected an armful of papers as well. As we scoured them for information, Simon's picture leapt off the page. We had no idea how the press had got hold of it but it was a clear message: my baby and I were in the public eye, whether we wanted to be there or not.

The other issue that was bubbling away in my head was the fact that I still hadn't seen my mum and dad. Mum was seriously ill with Multiple Systems Atrophy, a strain of Parkinson's Disease, and Dad had been her full-time carer for the best part of a year. Mum was mentally fit but struggled physically on a daily basis. She couldn't walk on her own any more and relied heavily on Dad to help with everything. Increasingly she only trusted Dad to help her with anything personal or physical. She would really have struggled to get down to London and the emotional journey would have been deeply distressing for her. Consequently neither of them was able to come down to be with me, and it was my brother and sisters who stepped into the parental role. Simon and I had visited my parents in May to tell them about my pregnancy and it had been wonderful to have the opportunity to share the grainy pictures of my first scan with Mum when she was still well enough to appreciate the good news.

I hated the fact that I couldn't have Mum and Dad there. In my head I understood that Mum was very ill and that Dad had to be with her, but in my heart I needed them. I was terrified by my situation and reverted instinctively to vulnerable-child mode. I needed to feel safe and protected and if I couldn't have

Simon, then I needed Mum and Dad. This was the worst thing I'd ever had to face and they weren't there. Dad was always at the end of the phone to talk to but Mum's illness meant that she found talking very difficult, so I couldn't even have that with her. Their absence was proving hard to handle or understand.

Instead, Mark, Deborah, Catherine and Ron took it in turns to be with me and to handle the mountain of questions and issues that were already beginning to surround me. They did everything within their power to help me with all that I threw at them. I had no idea of the stress and exhaustion they were coping with as I was so locked away in my thoughts that I couldn't see what they were doing around me. They were feeding me food I couldn't taste, and fielding phone calls from friends and people giving information from New York. They sat with me for hours on end trying to answer my ceaseless questions about why this had happened to me. It was unquestioning and unconditional sibling love.

It was Sunday 16 September and five days since the Twin Towers collapsed. Dad suggested on the phone that I should leave the house and go for a walk with the thought that fresh air would do me good. I didn't want to do this. The house had become my safe haven. I didn't know what would happen if I left it, and I definitely worried that if I went out no one would be at home if Simon called. I felt in control of what happened there, unlike the rest of my life. But my brother and sisters convinced me it was a good idea, and in spite of everything I did know that fresh air was good for me and the baby. It was the same with food. I didn't want to eat and I couldn't taste anything but I knew deep down that the baby needed it, and so I ate. Something primal was taking over. My instincts were growing stronger and I was beginning to develop a relationship with them every day.

So, my first outing was a trip to Kenwood House, which is a beautiful part of Hampstead Heath. The house was used in the film *Notting Hill*, with Julia Roberts dressed up in a Victorian lady's costume.

Deborah, Catherine, Mark, Ron and I walked around the grounds on a spectacular sunny Sunday morning. I looked up and there was the same blue sky and the distinct smell of autumn that had floated on the air on 11 September. But nothing could move the horror that sat in every cell of my body. I watched the other families enjoying a glorious Sunday morning walk and wondered if they had any idea what had happened to me. We had all seen the events unfolding in New York only a few days before and we all just carried on walking past each other.

I wanted to scream at everyone in the park, to stop them all and make them understand how much pain I was in.

To make it worse, Kenwood House is directly under the Heathrow flight path. I couldn't avoid the fact that whenever I looked up there were planes outlined against the clear blue sky. As I walked slowly up one of the hills I suddenly knew what to do. My intuition was tugging my head up to look at the sky. The planes that were a constant reminder of what had happened were also telling me to do something else.

'I have to go to New York,' I announced. The silence that fell across my family was one I was going to become more used to as I dropped bombshell decisions about my life, my baby and my way forward. It was the silence of people trying to work out how to manage me and my decision. It said, 'We hear what you're saying but you can't do it that way.' It also said, 'If we tell her no what will she do?' Luckily for my family this was one of the easier decisions to talk me out of because I had an overwhelming desire to do whatever was right for the baby. Although I was terrified of being a single parent I knew I really couldn't cope with losing the baby as well as Simon.

In the end I asked Simon's brother, Keith, and his best man, Pete, to fly to New York and find Simon and bring him home. Pete Willett, Simon, and another friend, Mike Blake, had been in the TA together. They were like the Three Musketeers. In 1992, they all decided to take time off work and do a tour with the army in Belize. While they were there they made a pact always to look out for each other and to bring each other home if the worst happened. Pete believed this was his opportunity to honour his agreement as Simon's best man. I also knew that if anyone could find Simon it was Pete, and that if he couldn't find him he would do everything he could and then tell me the truth.

Keith and Pete left for New York on Monday 17 September. When they arrived they were met by two police detectives who had been sent to New York from the UK to be their Family Liaison Officers for the duration of the trip.

The following morning, exactly a week after 11 September, Pete and Keith were taken to Pier 94. It sounded like a night-club but was, in fact, an enormous old warehouse on a pier on the lower west side of Manhattan Island. It was the centre of operations for the whole event of 11 September and where all the families could go for information.

They arrived at the front desk, which was housed behind wire fences plastered in the missing posters that had become the focal point for relatives' searches. There were hundreds of metres of photocopied faces with desperate pleas for missing loved ones. Pete and Keith began to realize the scale of loss that would unfold over the following weeks and months by the sheer number of those missing faces.

Once inside the pier, they were taken to one of the many small booths where they were briefed about the process that would follow. New York was treating the attacks as a murder inquiry, so they would have to register the victim's name and be interviewed by two New York detectives. Pete explained they were representing me because I couldn't fly due to the late stage of my pregnancy and they would be doing everything to find out what had happened. Simon wasn't registered as missing with the NYPD despite the police in the UK completing and submitting all this information. At the time the UK and US used different forms, which meant they had to register all the information again. Pete asked next to see the injured lists from the various hospitals around the Manhattan area. This was crucial as he knew it was the one hope I was clinging to.

'I'm sorry, sir, we have no one listed under the name of Turner.'

'Is there a possibility that he could be unidentified and in hospital?' Pete asked.

The detective took another glance at the lists on his computer screen. 'I'm sorry but all the injured are accounted for and named.'

I didn't know it at the time, but that was the moment one of my hopes died. Pete now knew that Simon was either trapped or dead. Suddenly the reason for his trip shifted. It was all made more emotional and shocking by the woman in the cubicle next to them. She had just been given the same news and let out a scream that stilled and silenced the entire vast space. It was the sound of heartbreak. The sound of hope being extinguished.

Eventually Pete composed himself again and asked, 'What can we do now, then?'

The detectives explained that in the event that Simon's remains were found they would need a DNA sample to match them. They asked if Pete could collect Simon's bags from the hotel and find a toothbrush or comb. Pete laughed out loud. Even in the darker moments he was able to find humour in the warm memory of his best friend. His nickname for Simon was 'Baldy'.

Once back outside, Pete and Keith took the opportunity to look around. There was a navy ambulance ship that dwarfed the pier, but it was empty. The city of New York was dealing with the dead, not the injured. Down the west side of the island was the most disturbing sight of all. Parked nose to tail for as far as they could see was a line of enormous articulated refrigerator trucks, perhaps sixty in all. Pete never knew if they were used but the sight of them underlined the sheer scale of the disaster and the reality of its after-effects.

By the end of the day Pete realized that his search was not going to have the ending I wanted. They'd visited the authorities, Family Liaison Officers and the Foreign Office. The last fireman had been brought out alive and there were no other reports from Ground Zero. The injured had all been accounted for. All the forms had been filled out. All identification had been provided. They'd done everything that could be done and with every line exhausted it was time to tell me that Simon was dead.

Pete called the house and spoke to Deborah.

Before coming home Pete and Keith were invited to the British Consulate's Remembrance Service for the UK victims. The service was to be televised around the world and everyone was wearing suits. Pete hadn't thought to pack a suit – his focus had been on finding Simon, not attending smart functions. So, surrounded by dignitaries and cameras, he stuck out like a sore thumb wearing a rather loud green Gap shirt. He laughed, knowing I'd be able to pick him out easily.

Afterwards the relatives were invited to a small reception, also attended by the world's great and good, including Tony Blair, Kofi Annan, New York Mayor Giuliani and Bill and Chelsea Clinton.

Pete was introduced to Tony Blair and in a moment of clarity asked him if he might do something for me.

'Please can you call Elizabeth in England? It would really mean something to know that the relatives are being thought about?'

'Oh yes, of course,' came the reply.

Pete rooted around in his shirt pocket trying to find a pen and paper, but it wasn't designed to hold a pen for the moment when the Prime Minister needed your number. In the end Tony Blair handed him both and he scribbled down my details.

I realized that Simon was dead on 20 September 2001. It's a date that is etched as deep in my memory as 11 September 2001.

I was about to fall asleep in my room when I heard the phone ringing somewhere in the house. I wanted to answer it because with Pete and Keith in New York any phone call could be them ringing to say they'd found Simon. I'm not sure I truly believed that would happen at this late stage but I hoped. I hoped more than I have ever hoped for anything in my life. But I couldn't answer the phone because of the press.

Deborah spoke to Pete and then waited for Mark to come back from the shops. They phoned Catherine, who was at home for an antenatal appointment, and explained the call they had just had from Pete and what they now needed to tell me before she could return. She was secretly relieved.

'I don't think my hormones could cope with this part,' she said. 'I'm more than happy for you to do it without me.'

Deborah then phoned Dad. She took the phone outside and explained what they were about to do. There were seven tree stumps at the bottom of the garden where Simon and I had cut down some Leylandii trees when we first bought the house. Deborah spent half an hour talking to Dad, walking across the cut trunks in a figure of eight. Up and down she weaved, in a pattern she'd used during childbirth to try to control a situation that frightened her. Now she was using the same technique to prepare for one of the most difficult conversations ever.

'You can do this really well,' Dad reassured Deborah. 'Tell her the truth. She has to understand now that Simon is dead.' It sounded quite brutal to Deborah, but she understood the loving intent behind his firmness. She had to make it clear to me that Simon was never coming home.

I came down from my sleep and went to sit on the steps outside the back door. Mark and Deborah came to join me. It was another beautiful autumn day that belied the disappearance of summer. I could see the three poplar trees that lined the bottom of my neighbour's garden swaying in front of me and I thought back to the time I'd told Simon I wanted to buy this house because of the beautiful trees at the back. I had visions of sitting in the back room holding my new-born baby with him, watching the wind in their branches.

'We've heard from Pete and Keith in New York,' Mark told me.

Deborah and Mark sat next to me, and Mark told his youngest sister that her husband was dead. I don't remember any of the words they used during that conversation and Deborah doesn't remember anything I said either. Out of the entire period this was the only moment that she can't remember at all. All those years we'd played together, fought with each other and tried to get each other into trouble with our parents. All those wonderful things you do as a family that you just take for granted. Sharing Christmas, walking, playing in the garden, going swimming, going on holiday and sneaking pinches in the back of the car. Nothing could have prepared us for having to share this as siblings. I could feel Deborah and Mark watching me as if they expected something to happen. I looked down and saw that I was wearing Simon's old gardening shoes. Should I break down and wail or collapse with grief? Should I be hysterical or scream or get angry with them for being the ones to tell me? But all I could think was – what shall I do now? In the silence that followed I became aware of music playing in the kitchen. It was Louis Armstrong singing 'What a Wonderful World'.

So Simon was dead. I never spoke to him after the first plane hit and he wasn't one of the people who left a message. I think he consciously made the decision not to call me. He would have seen other people making calls but I think his army experience would have given me a greater knowledge about what was going on around him. He knew what to do in smoke-filled rooms, with fire or in the dark in a dangerous situation. I am sure he would have switched into military mode and thought about the fact that I was seven months pregnant and that phoning me and telling me what was happening would have caused me a lot of distress. I can't imagine that he knew the images were being beamed all over the world at this point and that I was watching the entire event live in my office. Whether he knew he was going to die or not I believe he would have been thinking about what was best for me and the baby. He would have made the right decision for him with what he knew at the time. He loved me and his unborn child and he would have put us first and his own needs last. I often wonder whether I would have liked to have had that last moment together, but I honestly believe it would have been too painful for both of us. I believe that Simon died knowing all he needed to about my love for him. One more phone call wouldn't have added anything.

I didn't know exactly how Simon had died, but I knew he was dead. He wasn't coming home and at the age of thirty-three I was a widow and about to be a single parent. I didn't know what to do. I couldn't believe that our time together was over. The physical reaction to the news spread across my body. I instinctively wanted to curl up in a foetal position like my unborn child to escape from the pain in my heart. I could feel it beginning to break into a thousand tiny pieces. It was a deep, sad, slow, breaking apart, the cracks spreading around the space and moving across the heart so slowly that I could feel each single break. In its place I was left with a dark emptiness. Space. Nothing. Just a hole that had no bottom and no sides. It expanded out and attracted every sad and painful energy around it, magnifying the reality of Simon's death as if the pain grew on one side to balance the scale of love on the other. My life had stopped being normal and my heart would never be the same again.

Every year the first smell of autumn in the air reminds me of that conversation.

Chapter Five

After letting go of the hope, reality crashed in. Each morning I opened my eyes and I didn't want to wake up. For a very small moment in time I drifted from the beautiful world of sleep to consciousness and had to search my mind for my story. Then I found it. The truth hanging in the empty space of my heart.

I cried each time I woke up as the feeling of depression engulfed me again and I lay back on my pillow and desperately tried to return to sleep. It was the worst part of the day. Remembering that I was alone and that Simon wasn't coming home was unbearable. I thought of dying at that point because every time I woke up and remembered, I hated it, and if I killed myself I would never have to repeat this waking-up pattern that dragged me further into depression with each day I moved away from Simon's death. I didn't want to be there and I definitely didn't want to have to face my life as it was.

There were days when I really wanted to die. I felt that the only way to get rid of the crushing pain within me would be to be dead. I remembered how I used to walk home from work and think how great life was and wonder how anyone could fail to love it. But now I understood why people took their own lives. It was just to find peace. That was all.

I could see why people would choose to take drugs, or to drink. In the place that I found myself, the easiest and least painful solution would be to get high or drink myself into oblivion. Alternatively, I could go missing or have a nervous breakdown. I was now in the place where I had to make that choice. I felt hopeless and no one could help me. No one could say it would be all right because they had no idea that it would be. I needed someone in my corner, particularly as I was pregnant, saying, 'I'm here and I'm looking after you and it'll all be fine.' Instead everyone was saying, 'OK, we've lost the rule book.'

Grief's deep well of emotions is one of society's best-kept secrets. I had no idea how deep the well was. I fell into an abyss which was like the deepest, darkest trench at the bottom of a sea that no one has explored yet. The pressure, darkness and depth were too much for my mind and body to withstand and that was where I was taken. It was where all my worst fears about Simon's death were held. The place was physical and so dark that I didn't think I would ever see light again.

I had never known pain, grief, crying like it. I cried so deeply, I didn't believe it was possible. I hurt so much it was unimaginable and nobody could help me.

How could I carry all this emotion and look after a baby? I couldn't even look after myself and none of the traditional grief support appeared to be working. It didn't matter what I said, how angry I got, how much I cried and how much I asked for help, I was alone, empty inside and spiralling down. I felt as dead as Simon was.

My darkest fear in the abyss was that Simon had been one of the people who had chosen to jump from the building. I couldn't imagine how he must have felt if that was the better option. This was the part of my grief that brought me closest to breaking point. Was I prepared to face this fear or would it actually kill me?

During this time I felt I'd met my own soul. I felt my heart break, knew what it was like not to breathe, and what it felt like to die even though in reality it was an emotional, not physical death. I understood what living hell meant.

The weight of pain, emotion and fear pressed down on me so hard that I believed I was going to be crushed and that I would die anyway. Suicide would simply accelerate this and in a strange way I believed that it would help all the people around me who would no longer have to watch my pain or try to work out how to help me. I couldn't see beyond the blackness and could only feel the tight cold grip on my entire body. Every cell hurt, my brain was tight like an iron press, the panic and nausea never subsided, and I ached from vomiting. The need to scream, smash, break and cause huge destruction festered in my body, searching for an outlet. This railing against heaven and hell was exhausting and it raged like a caged wild animal. The necessity to hurt myself, to find something – anything – to block or release the excruciating pain and anger, was all-consuming. Where was I supposed to put energy at that level? Where was a box big enough and strong enough to hold it? Who could then take it off me?

The room where I eventually found myself was windowless and black, filled with cobwebs, dirt, evil, hate, anger, fury, revenge, emotionally ravaged bodies, pain. All my fears and demons were captured within the same four walls. I could find no way out. This room held the blueprints for the rest of my life's journey. They lay on the table and I looked at them all. Which path should I take? Which one was the easiest? Which one would take all of the horror away? Which was the quickest? Which one would eradicate all of the emotions immediately?

This was where I had to make my choice – drugs, drink, hatred, suicide? It would all be gone.

Or love, hope and the courage to go on? Theoretically that was the one I wanted, but standing in that black void I didn't believe I could manage the length of the journey carrying that wild lashing animal of emotion on my back without getting scratched and bitten to death anyway. They were all appalling choices. I was beginning to realize that even if I chose life, I might not make it. I understood that some people don't survive.

I had heard that in theory it takes two to three years to recover from a natural bereavement and about seven to recover from a complicated one. In my view and in my experience some people never recover. Instead they bury their emotion and run away from confronting it so that they can fit back in with everyone else. But grief sits and waits. You have to face it eventually.

It was a huge realization that I had all of this to deal with and that the choice was mine and no one else's. Unless you have visited that room, never judge someone. Only if you have stood in the dark and faced those choices does your soul know the courage that it took just to be there.

During this time I also felt overwhelming anger with people when they told me how I should feel, what I should do and what the textbooks told them about grief – even friends, family and counsellors. I was oblivious to their well-meaning ideas, which I knew wasn't fair, but I sat there and thought: how dare you think you know what it's like to be in this situation? If you haven't experienced such extremes of pain and despair, you couldn't possibly understand. You wouldn't even know that the deep trench existed. I had lost control of everything and I simply couldn't be dictated to like that. The truth was that time didn't make things normal, and life would never be the same again. Choice was the only control I had left.

There was a twenty-four-hour rota of friends and family making sure I had someone in the house with me in case I went into premature labour. My friend Jill was my first boss in London. On days when she was on duty we spent our evenings together sitting on the sofa and I talked to her about all the strange thoughts and questions that were whizzing around in my head. I found huge comfort in talking to her as her dad had died recently and she was dealing with her own grief. I never felt she was talking to help me, but that we were both exploring the endless questions that hung out there. One evening, I turned to Jill and admitted, 'I don't think I want to go on.'

'Then what's stopping you?' she asked. Jill never believed that avoiding the issue was right or that I would truly deliver on this option.

'I don't know what's stopping me,' I admitted, 'but the pain is so bad I can't help thinking that if I wasn't here it would go away.'

Jill didn't judge me. She didn't make a fuss about what I was saying and she didn't try to convince me not to do it. She allowed me to articulate my terrible fears, explored my thoughts with me and gave me the space to look at what I was considering. She didn't try to fix it or make it better. Her approach was exactly what I needed. I began to realize that my specific emotions had to be faced and acknowledged and I had to go searching. I looked anywhere I thought might help. I knew that my normal coping skills were hopelessly inadequate and that I needed something more powerful. I wanted to understand why I felt the way I did inside. Why did I need something bigger to be answered? Was it normal to be questioning my life so much? All I knew was that I felt something inside and I had to respond to it. I decided that I would do whatever was needed to answer these questions and calm my irrational thoughts.

Not one to do anything by halves, I worked with three different counsellors. One was from a bereavement charity, another was a therapist referred to me by my doctor and the last was a therapist who had been employed by Simon's company.

Each of them had a different style so two came to my house but one would only see me at her house in London as she felt it was good for me to get out. This made me very angry as it was so patronizing. I don't think she realized that because of what had happened I was doing nothing *but* getting out, sorting out the chaos.

Each of the counsellors I worked with was in their own way kind, gentle, compassionate and careful. I sat and talked. I told them about the trauma I felt inside, the questions going on in my head and the terror I had about my future. I cried and sobbed and exhausted myself trying to understand what had happened to me. I knew that what I was dealing with was extreme but, instead of acknowledging this, the people I saw seemed only able to look to their textbooks, and this approach was never going to work for me. I was definitely trapped in a parallel universe and I wanted answers and someone to blame for it all.

I'm not sure how many sessions I had with each one but after a while I knew I wasn't getting anywhere. What they did do was show me that my mind couldn't help me because it didn't have the capacity or frame of reference to deal with the experience. Instead I had to feel my emotions, allowing them to be as they were rather than fighting them, until I could absorb it all and accommodate it within me. Nothing had yet helped me with this. I was beginning to suspect that the way forward was to try everything and to eliminate whatever didn't work. Then maybe I would be left with what I did like.

I grilled friends and family for their beliefs and thoughts about my situation. What did they think had happened? Did they know anyone in a similar situation? How did they deal with it? I asked Catherine some very complex religious questions about life and the universe and she had to phone Dad for help as she was out of her depth.

I spent a lot of time talking to my dad too, trying to find out more about his faith and whether it helped him. He told me a story about when he was a boy. His mother died suddenly from food poisoning when he was only about thirteen years old. In those days the funeral was attended by adults only and it was considered best to shield children from the realities of death. It was a very difficult time for the family as his dad was left a widower with three children to bring up on his own. One day, my dad was ill off school in the house on his own. As he lay in his bed he heard the back door open and knew that his mum had just come into the house. He never heard the door open again for her to leave. Dad said that from that point on he always felt that his mum was with him and it brought him great comfort. He also realized that he wasn't scared of death because he could still feel his mum's presence. When Dad told me this story I felt relief and acceptance.

So, therapists were out and stories about spirituality, intuition and inner peace were in. It still looked like a very unstable framework to support my grief but that didn't seem to matter too much at this point. It felt right and that was my only internal compass.

Next I had a visit from the vicar of the local church. He was a wonderfully kind man who sat with me and drank cups of tea. I thought we were going to talk about the Christian faith and how it could support me. But instead he told me how his own faith was currently being tested since his little grand-daughter had been diagnosed with cancer of the eye. He explained that even as a vicar he had searched for an explanation as to why such a gorgeous little girl could be given something so big to deal with. He wanted to have the cancer himself because he had lived a lot of his life and it seemed unfair that she could possibly lose her sight at such a young age. The vicar explained that eventually he was able to trust in God. He had faith that there was a reason behind this situation. It was part of a bigger picture that couldn't fully be seen yet. He had found himself moving closer to God rather than further away.

I respected the vicar for sharing this story with me and although religion wasn't what I needed, I learnt something else. I found that I respected people who had felt something similar to the depth of the emotion that was crushing me, rather than just reading a theory in a book.

*   *   *

66

I was also given a book by a friend who had found it useful during a difficult divorce. It struck a chord and began to feel like a lifeline. I recognized the words in *Conversations with God* by Neale Donald Walsch, and liked the ideas that he put forward about spirituality rather than religion. In one particular section, the author asks whether the information in the book is really true and God replies, 'If it is true or not, isn't this a good way to live your life anyway?'

I read the words and immediately grasped the resonance with my own choices. If they looked strange to others or made them uncomfortable, did that make the choices bad? I realized that if they were helping me, that was good enough at this stage.

The next part of my search came from an avenue I had definitely not expected. Simon had an Australian friend called Chris who he'd met on the Honourable Artillery Company (HAC) New Recruits course. The HAC recruited Simon but Chris decided it all looked too much like hard work and, unbeknown to Simon in a different group, decided not to sign up. Simon did all the training and Chris enjoyed going with him to all the balls and socializing. I had met Chris briefly in a pub with Simon the summer before he died and Chris and I had started chatting about religion and our beliefs. He was interested in the philosophy behind Tarot cards, and although this wasn't something I knew about we enjoyed a conversation about what we believed in. About four weeks after Simon's death I had a phone call from Chris explaining that his father had died and he was coming to London for the funeral. He had written an account that he felt had somehow come from Simon and he believed it was important to give it to me. But he was very sensitive and understood that perhaps I might not want to see it.

I didn't hesitate. I wanted to see and do everything that was presented to me and then decide what felt right. Chris and Simon had a strong connection that endured in spite of their geographical separation and I was intrigued by what he was bringing. Some of my friends, however, weren't so enthusiastic about the visit. I began to realize that my search did look mad to others and was a cause for concern. I was scared that the people I loved were judging my choices to the point where I started to wonder whether they were right or wrong. I reminded myself of my anchor – Simon in the World Trade Center – and his decision over whether to stay in the building or jump. It wasn't about right or wrong but bad or worse. My choices, by comparison, were based on looking mad or going mad. I decided to take the options that might lead me out of my inner madness and hoped that my family and friends would understand.

Chris arrived at the house with all Simon's joie de vivre and sociability and a healthy dose of Australian directness. He gave me the piece of writing that he felt had come to him from Simon a few days after 11 September. He told me that he didn't need or expect any response from it but he knew he had to offer me the option of reading it.

I'm not sure what I felt before I read it. I knew that Chris and Simon had been very close, and I was touched by the care and sensitivity with which he'd approached me about it. But I was sceptical nonetheless. This is what he had written:

It was evening and I had a sudden feeling of contact that was Simon talking about the events, coming through quite clearly considering how busy my mind is these days.

Here is the text of the communication:

We were getting ready for the start of the delegates arriving at the conference; there was the usual late start as we waited for the various people to arrive. It was soon after 8.45 that we heard the slam and thunder of what was the first plane hitting the building, but we had no knowledge of where. Soon after that the fire started and then we began to panic as smoke infiltrated the room, rising up through the vents. We didn't think we were in that much danger as the sprinkler system kicked in and the smoke disappeared, but it wasn't long before we realized that there was much more and we became aware of the heat coming up through the floors. We knew things were serious and began to wonder how they would reach us up so high. It was then that we realized what was happening as we saw the other plane fly into the second building. That was when we really panicked, not from what might happen to us, but from what we had seen. It seemed like the seconds were ticking by slowly. I tried to remain calm but was sick with fear like everyone else. I tried to crack a few jokes – funny nobody laughed. At this time there was no fire actually reaching us, so although we were very worried and frightened, we did think that we would be rescued, despite the enormity of what we had witnessed.

We sat in silence waiting – one woman was sick, she was so scared. Then there was the noise, the rumble as we felt the roof above us crashing down. It was only seconds and then it was all over and here I am now.

CHRIS: *How soon did you realize that you were dead?*

SIMON: *Immediately, I could see all of the devastation disappearing below me and I was just 'there', not on anything, just there, witnessing the building fall away. I don't remember any others while I experienced this, it all happened so fast.*

CHRIS: *Do you know you are dead?*

SIMON: *Yes.*

CHRIS: *What are you hanging around for?*

SIMON: *I want to let Elizabeth know that I am well and thinking of her. I want her to know that I am OK and that this is my time to move on. There is no reason, it just is my time. I love her and want her to know that I will always watch over her and our baby, wherever they may go in life.*

CHRIS: *Where do you go from here?*

SIMON: *Time does not exist here, so I have no future plans as such, things will just be as they unfold. This place is serene, but the turmoil of the last few days is in my thoughts also. I guess they will pass in time, but apart from that I can give you no hint as to my journey. All I know is that it is long and encompasses many passages through experiences from my past, reliving them, facing the mistakes and joy I have brought to others – many lessons to learn.*

CHRIS: *Are you in contact with the spirits of others that have passed over?*

SIMON: *Yes and no.*

The communication was interrupted at this point by Suzie [Chris's wife] coming to bed, but Simon was beginning to tell me how he was alone, but also vaguely aware of the others around him.

The writing itself didn't have a huge impact on me. Mum had always told me that once people died, their spirit lived on. So fundamentally, I didn't need to decide about my belief in spirits. But whether or not the writing came from Simon, I was aware of an overwhelming feeling of reassurance. It certainly would have been like him to start cracking jokes even in such a desperate situation. For the first time, I felt a glimmer of a connection with him. Not being able to talk to or see the man I loved was the hardest thing. But for the first time I felt that someone had shown me Simon might be around.

I was still talking on my own at night. I wasn't sure whether I was talking to God, energy, space, angels or whatever name you place on the mysterious 'thing' that we hope is out there at these times. I called it The Universe simply because this felt less like a little man with a white beard and more like a dynamic energy that was greater than anything I could comprehend. I don't honestly believe that I thought anything would come of my conversations but I did feel that it was worth a try.

It was deeply significant to me that in the end I did ask for help. I had always been so fiercely independent but for the first time I accepted that my resources didn't stretch far enough to be able to do this on my own. I had no idea what form it would come in, but I knew I needed help.

The night after I read the piece of writing from Chris I dreamt about Simon and he smiled at me.

Chapter Six

On the Friday after the events in New York, my friend Jane Perks announced that she didn't think it was in my best interests to have my baby through the NHS because of the press interest.

With this in mind, she contacted Channel 4 and talked to Peter Meier, the HR Director, about the fact that she was arranging for me to have my baby privately. She told him that all my friends were going to club together to pay for this and she was talking to a number of people to see if they wanted to contribute. Channel 4 saw this as their opportunity to support me, and offered to pay for the whole thing. It was an incredible gesture.

Next, Jane tried to contact Mr Gillard, the obstetrician she had used when she went privately with her second child after the complicated birth of her first son.

'He is the only man for the job,' she told me.

Mr Gillard was on holiday so Jane was eventually passed to the American owner of the Portland Hospital. Jane explained my circumstances to her.

'Elizabeth is here. Her suite is booked and she can be here any time,' the owner replied.

Jane was amazed by the speed and generosity of people when

helping someone in need. When Mr Gillard returned from his holiday she asked whether it would be possible for him to take me onto his books at this late stage. He didn't bat an eyelid, but quietly admitted to Jane that it was going to be very hard. 'But I'll do everything I can to make sure that Elizabeth has the best experience possible!' He felt it was a unique opportunity to truly help somebody. Not everyone could have done it, but he knew he could manage the delicate balance between emotion and efficiency.

I trusted Jane's choice of obstetrician but Mr Gillard wasn't sure I would necessarily feel comfortable with him. By contrast, I knew that my intuition was working hard on my behalf and I was learning to trust it. I first met him on 19 September, when I still thought that Simon was missing, not necessarily dead. I knew the minute we met that he would look after me. I also knew immediately that Simon would have liked him too.

'I'll be your stand-in dad and your stand-in husband throughout the whole process,' he promised me. 'It'll all be fine and there's no reason that you can't have a normal delivery. We can manage the rest of this without any problems.'

He explained that he would normally meet a client up to eleven times during a pregnancy and therefore suggested that we met every week up to the birth of my baby. That way, after eight or so appointments, we'd have established a relationship before the due date. My visits to him were all about support and encouragement. Jane came with me to every one and he talked to us both while carrying out all the usual antenatal checks, reassuring me that the baby and I were both doing well.

At the end of every check-up there was a tearful hug for everyone which was also reassuring. These were not just medical visits but emotional ones too. I felt I was in very good hands with this special man who cared so deeply about me and my baby. I trusted him, which under the circumstances was incredibly important.

I demonstrated this very early on, by confessing some of my deepest fears about the baby.

'I'm panicking about something,' I told him. 'In the first two weeks after I got pregnant but didn't know, I went to Twickenham to the rugby with Simon, my sister and brother-in-law and then on to dinner in London afterwards and we all got very, very drunk. Will my baby be all right?' Mr Gillard laughed.

'Elizabeth, most babies are conceived in this state. Everything will be fine!'

He was so non-judgemental about all the situations I talked to him about.

'This panicking is very normal too,' he told me. 'You're reacting like any mum in the late stages of pregnancy.' He held my hand every step of the way.

Sometimes, when I sat in his office, I wondered at how exceptionally perceptive he was. He seemed to know about my latest worries before I'd even told him. In fact there was an extraordinary network of support going on silently behind me. I talked to my sisters who told Jane who rang Mr Gillard who then knew just what was on my mind at my next antenatal visit. It looked like he was a mind reader from where I was sitting.

There was one visit that Mr Gillard couldn't help me with and that was a scan to check the baby in its final weeks. I heard my baby's heartbeat on the monitor, knowing that my husband's heart had now stopped. The cruel juxtaposition of the birth of a baby and the death of a father inspired and crushed me in equal measure.

I asked Jane to be with me at the birth. It was something I'd thought about long and hard. Mum was too ill, Catherine was heavily pregnant herself and by the time of the delivery Deborah would have gone home after being with me for nearly two months. Jane was one of my oldest friends, she had children of her own, and she'd introduced me to Simon. She'd also made all the arrangements with Mr Gillard. She'd done so much to help me and I knew she would do everything in her power to help again at my baby's birth. I couldn't think of a better person for the job.

While all this was going on, there was a mountain of bureaucracy to wade through. As well as the continual liaising between the Metropolitan Police and New York, I was dealing with frozen bank accounts and financial complications. I still had the press at my front door, on the phone and hunting down friends, relatives and neighbours for comments. My life felt surreal and every week I felt the sense of dislocation more acutely with each new experience I had to face.

Eleven days after the Twin Towers collapsed I went to the American Embassy to swear an affidavit confirming that Simon was in the World Trade Center so that I could be issued with a death certificate. Keith drove me down to Grosvenor Square where I had to take all the documents by hand to be stamped with the American seal. The embassy then submitted them to the American government, who sent out the certificates.

It was unprecedented to be given a death certificate so soon when you didn't have a body. Amanda told me that the complex procedure had been put in place because there were so many people making false claims. They apparently saw the opportunity to change their identity, go missing or claim compensation, and so the authorities, despite having to deal with such an enormous disaster, were being forced to sift out the people who were really alive. I couldn't begin to think about someone who would put themselves or others into those towers when all I wanted was to bring Simon out.

As Keith and I inched our way between the concrete crash barriers, past armed police and through the X-ray machines, I felt very bleak and also very sick. Simon hadn't benefited from any of this security and all the ostentatious measures felt token to me. The horse had long since bolted. I should have been picking out fluffy toys and hanging up pastel-coloured mobiles. But instead of enjoying the last few weeks of my pregnancy, I was trying to prove to a foreign embassy that my husband really had been in a building that had just been destroyed by terrorists on the other side of the world – so that I could receive a death certificate I didn't want. What I really wanted to prove was that he hadn't been there at all.

When Pete returned from New York and told us about his conversation with Tony Blair, we all laughed at his boldness. I was very touched by what he had tried to arrange but never expected anything to happen. So when I was lying on my bed one afternoon pretending to have an afternoon nap and Catherine popped her head around the door to say that Cherie Blair would be calling a bit later, I assumed it was all a big joke.

'Seriously, she really is phoning you!' Catherine explained that Cherie had been in contact with my Family Liaison Officer, and Amanda had called Catherine to check that it would be OK.

We stalked around the house for the rest of the afternoon, jumping when the phone rang and shouting at friends and family to get off the line.

Eventually I found myself sitting cross-legged on my bed, talking to the Prime Minister's wife about pregnancy, going to the Portland, parent-craft classes and maternity nurses. She was warm and genuine, and at the end she promised me tea at Number 10 with Baby Turner and Leo. My life had officially moved into a parallel universe.

I had another surreal experience, going to John Lewis with my sisters to buy the equipment for the baby. Simon and I had chosen most of what we'd need together, but we hadn't actually bought it. Jane pointed out that when the baby was born everyone would want to send presents and gifts – a way to mark the happy occasion after so much devastation. This would be wonderful, but I didn't want to end up with 400 babygros and bibs! So she cleverly suggested setting up a baby list. In the light of this, Catherine, Deborah and I arranged another trip to John Lewis to sort it out. We were about to discover that bereavement, pregnancy hormones and shopping in the West End are a recipe for disaster.

I wandered around the store, remembering being there with Simon only a few weeks earlier, and could barely breathe at the horror of it all. I could see happy couples looking at baby things together and felt so huge, shocked and furious that I really could have punched anyone who said the wrong thing. The world had never seemed as unfair to me as it did on that shop floor. But we had to do this, and somehow I had to pull myself together. Even when I spied the Mamas and Papas buggy that Simon had promised he would find for me, I looked away, took a deep breath and walked straight past.

I was fading rapidly and growing paler and paler with the enormity of the task and the effort it took to choose everything. Deborah knew it was a huge requirement but she also knew she didn't want to make this trip again. So she took over and, with me and Catherine trailing in her wake, picked up all the different items and told me what I needed to have. With the help of the wonderful staff, we had soon picked out bed linen, clothes, monitors, buggies and all the little things a new baby needs.

It should have been a happy, special time, and Catherine and Deborah couldn't have tried harder to make it easy and fun. But for me there wasn't an ounce of joy to be had and I was consumed by grief and sadness.

As we left the shop, Catherine turned to me. 'At least that's all done and we don't have to go back again,' she said, trying to find some comforting words in a day that had made them impossible. That was it. The lid of the pressure cooker was off, and the emotion of the day poured out. My poor sisters had no choice but to bundle me into the back of the car and navigate themselves back through the one-way systems of London with me sobbing uncontrollably on the back seat. There was nothing that could be said.

A few days later I received a call from John Lewis.

'Mrs Turner, we just wanted to let you know that everything on your list has now been bought,' the manager told me.

I was staggered. The baby hadn't even been born and everything had gone!

'In fact,' the manager continued, 'one of your friends, a Mrs Llewellyn-Bowen, has bought the entire list.'

I had to laugh. This was so Jackie and so precisely what Simon had loved about her. He was godfather to Jackie and Laurence's youngest daughter, Hermione, and they were very close friends. The wonderful things that friends did at these times kept my heart open despite its desire to die.

It was also at about this time that my sisters and Jane were party to a difficult conversation with Mr Gillard.

'Suicide!' he said. 'If this woman goes back to her home with a new baby and no support at all she will not survive.'

As a result it was decided that I needed a maternity nurse for three months after my baby was born. At least then there would be someone in the house to help me cope with the loneliness, exhaustion, fear and of course the day-to-day requirements of a new-born baby. Deborah started to contact all the agencies to find someone they could trust to be with me.

I was too deep in my grief and trauma to notice the love and care that were being exhaustively arranged around me. I was struggling not to drown under all the responsibilities of Simon's death and the sheer weight of my emotions.

Through my exhausted tears I started to beg for help again when I was in my bedroom on my own.

'I want you back,' I pleaded at night. 'I can't imagine my life without you, and I'm so scared of being on my own. I don't know how I'm going to move forward and I'm terrified of all of my emotions. Please help me. I'm so scared that I won't get through this and yet I know I must for the sake of our baby. I don't want it to be born into a bitter, angry and ruined home.

I have a responsibility to sort myself out but I don't know how to deal with what I'm feeling. I need help.'

Jan Kirsop Taylor arrived to be interviewed with a big bag of leeks from her friend's allotment, and sat on the sofa and talked to us all about her life and what she'd done. She had immense presence. She was calm but also slightly unnerving, as though she knew something we didn't. Above all she was wonderfully motherly and made me feel warm, safe and protected in the short time she was with us.

We showed her around the house, which was in chaos. Simon and I hadn't finished decorating and so many visitors had lived and stayed in it since his death that there were lots of people and bags around. Jan didn't notice any of this or if she did she never mentioned it. Deborah did almost all the talking and I sat very quietly and listened and watched. At the end of the interview I told Jan that I'd already tried a number of different things to help with my grief but nothing was working, and she told me about the holistic courses and coaching she was involved in. She explained that she wanted to help me work out how to look after my baby myself. Deborah liked Jan and even felt that she could probably help me in other ways. I trusted Deborah. The decision was made. Jan was going to be my maternity nurse.

I immediately felt that Jan could relate to what I was going through. Her husband had died from throat cancer ten years previously and she'd been left with three sons to bring up in a financially challenging situation. During that period she'd taken her own long journey through grief. She'd started to look to complementary therapies for support, beginning by learning massage therapy, and as her interest developed so did her qualifications. She trained to be an aromatherapist and was then introduced to the spiritual healing technique. She soon set up her own business and started regularly seeing and working with clients. Through an interest in all things spiritual she explored colour therapy, visualization, meditation, past-life regression and psychic skills, and was eventually introduced to Reiki, a Japanese healing technique.

It had been a sunny Tuesday when Jan took the train down to London to register with an agency for a job as a maternity nurse. But, she carefully explained to them, she didn't want any old maternity nursing job. She wanted to work with someone in a special situation that would allow her to pull together everything she knew. It was only when she got home that she discovered what had been happening to the world that day. The day that Jan enrolled at the agency was 11 September 2001.

PART II
BECOMING

Chapter Seven

Jan arrived a little like Mary Poppins. She came in a small white car with a small bag and immediately set to work in the house. She looked at all the unopened baby equipment and I half expected her to say 'Spit Spot'.

'Why has none of this been opened yet?' She knelt down and started to rip it all open. She washed bedding, set up the cot and buggy and read instructions about how things worked. The sterilizer was set up in the kitchen and suddenly there was lots of home-cooked food. Jan was like a tornado and there was a different vitality about everything. She had come to show me that a baby would bring a new energy into the house, that life was always moving and I needed to start recognizing what was about to happen.

It was Ron's birthday the day after Jan arrived.

'Are you going to make Ron a birthday cake?' she asked. Catherine and I just laughed. We weren't renowned for our Domestic Goddess tendencies. So Jan discovered that he liked fruitcake and set about making one. It was a way of showing us that it was fine to celebrate despite the situation. There was a shout from the kitchen.

'Can I use Simon's whisky for the cake we're making? I know he won't mind.'

'Of course!' I shouted back. 'I won't be drinking it.' A moment later, my brain registered the words she'd used. I must have been mistaken. Yet it was undeniably true that I felt much calmer with Jan in the house. Her presence was peaceful and tranquil, even though she was constantly busy sorting out baby things and cooking. The house was being put into order after all the chaos and I liked it.

A few days later a Special Delivery package arrived in the post. It contained Simon's death certificates. I held them and looked at them, and although I knew they would help me sort out a lot of my finances, they were confirmation that Simon was dead and I hated them. Jan came in and saw that I was crying.

'What is it?' she asked, and I showed her. I was shaken by the reality of something I could hold that recorded the date, place, time and manner of Simon's death. It was really shocking to read the word 'homicide'. That was murder, and even though I knew Simon had been killed by terrorists, for some reason I had never put the event into the 'murder' category. How had my life grown so out of control? How could I begin to make sense of it? Jan looked at me and held my hand.

'They're just pieces of paper, Elizabeth. They don't change the reality of what you already know and they don't change the reality of the love that you feel for Simon. Look at them simply as information and the emotion will settle into where it all was before.' The drama fell away from the moment and I put the pieces of paper on the table so that Ron and I could deal with the financial complications later.

Jan and I talked and talked before my baby was born. I knew I'd found the source of information I needed and I wanted to learn as much as I could. I asked her everything I could possibly think to ask. I felt she was an encyclopaedia that I had access to for three months and it was up to me to get as much information from her as I could before she left.

'I want you to tell me everything you know,' I pleaded.

'I can't do that,' said Jan. 'You can only ask me questions when you're ready to hear the answer. It has to be your wish to hear the answers, not my wish to give them.'

It was during my first week with Jan that I started to see light in the tunnel. It wasn't much but I didn't care. Someone had lit a match and in the blackness that tiny, flickering light was everything.

We worked together making lists of contact details, people that Jan needed to know in case of emergencies, such as plumbers, insurance companies and builders. She met the friends I was close to and we talked about who I might choose to be godparents. Jan made me put the new pram in the car to see how it fitted, and we put it together and took it apart until I was used to it. She made me sleep with the Moses basket in my bedroom. She was helping to organize me when, left to my own devices, I would have hidden under my duvet cover. Simon had been a Sergeant Major in the TA and I felt he'd passed some of his skills on to Jan to sort me out. And all this time we talked. I bombarded her with questions about Simon's death – why did it happen? Was there a reason for it? Was there a lesson for me to learn? I listened to new perspectives about how the universe worked and discovered they were ideas I felt comfortable with.

Jan was kind, gentle and understanding. She told me everything the way it was, dealing only with the truth and facts. I loved her approach and when I looked at the car wreck of my life I believed she had been sent to help me. My knowledge of the spiritual and holistic was basic, but I'd enjoyed a few conversations with Mum about it as she was interested in aromatherapy, reflexology and massage. She also loved the idea of angels and told me that she always asked for a guardian angel to look after me and my brother and sisters when we were away. It felt like Mum had been right and I had been given a guardian angel, particularly as she couldn't be with me during this difficult time.

It was Saturday 10 November and the next day was Remembrance Sunday. 11.11.01. Such a poignant date. But it was also the day my baby was due to be born. When I realized this I knew I didn't want that to happen. I said to Jan that I didn't want this to be my child's birthday for the rest of its life. I was adamant that it should have its own name and its own birthday.

'OK, so we need to make sure the baby doesn't come,' she said. 'We need to keep busy.'

So the next day I took her in the car around Muswell Hill and showed her all the sights and sounds of my community. We parked the car so I could show her where Sainsbury's was, the bank, the post office, Marks & Spencer's food hall. All the important things in life! We walked past the local Odeon cinema which was screening a preview of the new Harry Potter film before it was officially released later in the week. Jan looked at me and said, 'Let's go and see it.'

'What if I go into labour while we're in the cinema?' I asked nervously.

'There's no way you'll go into labour while we're watching the film!' Jan exclaimed.

I didn't know how Jan could be so certain about everything at this stage but we watched the whole film and the baby didn't move a muscle. Safely back at home, I then spent an hour or so calmly explaining to distressed friends and family where I had disappeared to for nearly four hours.

Over the next couple of days, with the baby still quite happy where it was, I went to see Mr Gillard. It was miraculous that I had managed to see the full term of my pregnancy. But he believed that if I had to wait any longer I might become stressed and agitated, so he suggested an induction so that I would know when it was going to happen. In addition, Mr Gillard was able to choose his team of people for the day, and was also booked to go on holiday on the following Friday, so we had to bring the baby into the world before then because I didn't want anyone else to do it. My baby clearly wasn't ready to come out into all this chaos so it sat calm and still until it was induced. The date was booked for 14 November.

I stood in the room where my baby would be born and felt sick with fear. I was about to give birth to my child on my own and I was absolutely petrified by my place in the world. I looked at Jane and burst into tears. At precisely that moment the door opened and in walked two nurses. They swooped into the room, took one look at my despair and sadness and rushed over to hug and reassure me. They told me who they were and who was going to look after me, and that I had nothing to worry about. I began to feel some of my fears slide away. Then Breda, my midwife, walked in. She explained that her shift was from

8 a.m. to 8 p.m. but that she'd already decided she would stay with me for as long as it took for me to give birth.

So there it was. Within five minutes of my fears enveloping me I was presented with my team of people for the day. Jane Perks, my friend; Mr Mick Gillard, obstetrician; Breda, my midwife; and Sister Therese Hurl and Sister Ray Fagan, the nurses to support me. The stage was set and I felt calmer and safer.

I was beginning to understand that in the worst circumstances I was still being shown on a daily basis that I would be supported and looked after. I had my family, Jan had arrived, I had friends who were willing to be with me on a twenty-four-hour rota, I had the midwifery team at the Portland and Mr Gillard, I had Channel 4 and I had Jane. When I looked at my fear from the outside I was able to see how much I was being held in a place of safety. If only I could trust the process and have faith that everything would work out.

At 8 a.m. Mr Gillard began the process of inducing the baby's birth. Once the action started I felt much calmer. The experience was out of my hands and it was going to happen whether I liked it or not, so I might as well relax into it.

There were plenty of comings and goings throughout the day from Mr Gillard and the other medical staff. I was checked, monitored, injected and reassured by many people even outside the normal routines of the day. During the afternoon I was monitored by Breda and watched weekday afternoon programmes such as *A Place in the Sun* and *Countdown*. Mr Gillard came in and out between his Caesarean appointments. At one stage he completed a Caesarean, came down to my room to check on me, watched a bit of *Countdown* with Jane and me and successfully completed the conundrum. The word 'Jellyfish' will always be our code for the day that he was my surrogate husband! After that he went off again to do another Caesarean. He was a busy, talented and wonderfully kind man.

At 9 p.m. he returned.

'OK, Elizabeth, it's time to do all the hard work now. This is why it's called labour.'

'I've changed my mind. I don't want to do this any more,' I exclaimed. Mr Gillard immediately pulled up his jumper to show me the T-shirt he was wearing. It showed a cartoon pregnant woman lying on a bed saying, 'I have changed my mind!' Perfect. He knew what I was thinking as well. He was definitely the man for the job. Jane held my hand tightly and we both knew we'd do this together. I trusted her implicitly.

At 10.37 p.m. on 14 November 2001 my son was born. When he was placed in my arms it felt natural and right, as if that were simply how it was meant to be.

Jane and Mr Gillard brought in champagne and we all had a glass and everyone cried. 'This is what Simon would have done,' Mr Gillard announced, and he was right. He kept his thoughts to himself then, but he was desperately sad that I would be on my own to watch my son grow up.

I remember thinking, 'Oh my God, I have to look after him now.' My emotions were all over the place. After everything we'd both gone through he'd arrived safely. We were together despite what had been stacked against us. I was exhausted, in shock, surprised, happy . . . I was so delighted that my baby was healthy, and it was lovely for me that he was a boy because Simon and I had chosen a boy's name on the Sunday before he died. We never chose a girl's name.

'I'd like you all to meet William Simon Turner,' I said through my tears. William, not Simon. He should never replace Simon or feel he had to live up to him.

Mr Gillard came up to see me a day later. I was sitting in bed holding William who was asleep in my arms and we sat together for a while. I needed to thank him for everything he'd done.

I knew the enormity of what Mr Gillard had created for me during this awful time. There had always been the potential for the birth to be traumatic enough to affect the beginning of the relationship between William and me. The whole event had been staged with enough military precision to make even Simon proud. Mr Gillard and Jane's plan had worked and I knew they'd started our life together in the most positive way possible despite the horror around us. I looked at him and our eyes filled with tears. 'I'll never forget what you've done for me,' I said. A very special bond had been created between us and I knew we would forever be connected by our shared experience on that frosty day in November.

The days in hospital were much easier for me than the nights. I had nurses coming in and out, visitors to talk to, presents and cards to open, food to eat and most of all a baby to bathe, feed, hold and talk to. It was easy to be busy and avoid the devastation that was lurking behind the joy of William arriving.

But at night in the hospital when everyone had left and the post stopped coming, the building went quiet and dark. Then my fears and sadness came flooding back and I couldn't hold it in any more. It was like a tidal wave bursting through the flimsy barriers I'd erected and pinning me down under the weight of emotion. Again, I couldn't breathe. I could barely hold myself up under the burden of sadness. It was so strong and suffocating that even William couldn't reach me. It felt powerful enough to kill me, and I didn't dare lose control in case I couldn't pull myself back. But I realized that the more I fought the current the more it dragged me down. I had to learn to let go and let it wash through me until the waves had subsided. It took huge courage to trust in this process and it terrified me.

One night I was sitting on my bed talking to my brother on the phone. I was trying to be good for William by feeding him, changing him and getting him to sleep, but when I didn't satisfy him it all felt too much. My brother asked, 'Are you OK?' and I lost it. All my anger came out and I screamed and shouted and cried and cried. The next thing I knew one of the midwives had rushed into the room. She took William off to the nursery and then came straight back into my room to hug me. I don't know who she was as she was on the night shift and I'd never met her before and to this day I don't know her name. But maybe she was another guardian angel, sent, as Mum said, to help me in my darkest times. She held me until my sobbing calmed and subsided, and then we held hands and talked. She told me to ring at any time during the night and she would come. I never stopped being astounded by the kindness of strangers after Simon's death.

Chapter Eight

Everyone told me it would all feel better once the baby arrived as I'd have a routine and something to keep my mind occupied. That much was true but my emotions didn't change. It was hard work when William was born and to be honest, at that stage, all he provided me with was a framework, something I couldn't avoid doing and something that made me get up and out. I loved him because he was my baby but all I could think of was trying not to fall into the great abyss of grief, to protect William from my emotions and to stop everything else from falling down around me.

Every day William was beginning to look more and more like Simon. He was born with Simon's eyes and facial shape. I have chocolate-brown eyes but Simon's were so dark they were almost black. William's eyes began to change from the blue he was born with and it wasn't long before they were the same colour as his father's. They were piercing and defined, as if they looked right inside you. One of my friends said, 'At least we know Simon's the father,' which I thought was very funny. I loved the connection between Simon and William. There is a real bond between mums and sons and although I had to create that with William on a practical level, I knew that he and I were going to be very close. I also instinctively felt that from

September when Simon died to November when William was born, father and son had met and connected. The three of us would be entwined for the rest of our lives.

On 29 November, only two weeks after William was born, the National Memorial Service was held in Westminster Abbey. I was exhausted, grieving and angry, not to mention ravaged by the hormones flying around my body. Leaving William at home and facing such a huge task felt like a cruel joke. But there was never really any doubt about my going. Simon's body hadn't been recovered and I wasn't sure it ever would be so this might be as close as he and I ever got to a funeral. William was strong and well and I knew I could leave him safely in Jan's care. It would also give me the opportunity to invite the people who were closest to me and Simon to come too. For the first time we could all acknowledge Simon's death rather than focusing on me and the baby.

In spite of all this it was going to be my first day away from William and although I'd been terrified of what to do with him when I left hospital I was now terrified of being without him for any period of time. I was starting to feel the powerful unconditional love of motherhood and the cord that connected us was growing stronger by the day. I loved this little baby so much and combined with the love I had for his father and the grief of his loss I felt like I was about to explode or at the very least cry for ever.

As the day approached Jan picked up on the emotions around the house and gently asked me, 'Would you like to try a Reiki session tonight?'

We had talked about Reiki and spirituality since she'd arrived but I hadn't tried it. I didn't know what to expect and was very nervous in case it didn't work. What would I do then? I was also worried in case something awful happened. It was an area I had little information about other than what I'd talked to my mum about. But I had read about voodoo and Ouija boards. What if I opened things up that I couldn't put back? What if I met evil, or my crying never stopped?

On the other hand, I was at a dead end. I trusted Jan and I knew she'd been here before and wouldn't do anything I didn't want to. I decided the time was right to try something different.

We put William to bed and Jan assured me he wouldn't disturb us. I had no idea how she could make this promise but William never did wake up in any Reiki session I did with her. I was always completely amazed by this.

First, Jan asked me to sit on a chair in my bedroom. I was expecting something more symbolic or magical but she explained that she would only do a short Reiki session to give me a taster of it. Jan then explained a little more about Reiki. It is an ancient healing method from Tibet, which was rediscovered in Japan in the nineteenth century. It is a natural and simple healing method where universal energy is transferred through the hands of a Reiki practitioner into the body of the receiver. The Reiki method vitalizes the client's life force and balances the energies in the body. She told me she was going to create some energetic protection and support for me to use when I was at the memorial service the next day. I sat down and Jan told me to relax and simply be in the moment. I didn't know how to do that but decided that the next best thing was to close my eyes. There was some Reiki music on in the background and I could feel myself relax just slightly. To the naked eye it would have been barely discernible but I felt it. I also felt a little calmer. Again, it was a tiny move on the continuum but the combined experience was enough for me to know that something was happening.

Jan began to talk in a very calm and soothing voice. She explained that she was connecting to a universal energy and that she would place her hands on the various chakra points around my body through which she would channel energy. She told me that the Reiki energy might go into my body at one point but it would then travel to the place where it was most needed.

I felt pretty sceptical at this stage. I could hear the words but they didn't register with me as anything but New Age. I thought I probably had to put up with that bit in order to move on to the next stage. But I was also aware that my intuition was telling me to stay in the experience. I was unsure what the benefit might be but I did feel calm.

Jan then explained that she could see a male figure who was strong both physically and emotionally and that he had the energy of a soldier or a warrior. In the visualization he brought me a long red cloak to wear. It was made of a very heavy material which would provide me with courage and protection throughout the following day. Jan described the energy of the figure as similar to that of someone like John of Gaunt. I had never done a visualization before but I could see the figure in my mind and I could see the cloak too. I was completely out of my comfort zone, and the session felt strange, but for a very brief moment I felt a little less attached to my grief. Afterwards Jan handed me a crystal to hold in my pocket at all times the next day.

The following morning I prepared very carefully. I woke up feeling really nervous, and my sick feeling was back. But it was an important day, and I knew how much Simon would have loved it. He was a hero to me and I wanted to make him proud of my strength and courage. So I put on a suit and applied make-up for the first time since he'd died. I looked in the mirror and there I was: Elizabeth who was married to Simon and worked at Channel 4. I was intrigued. I looked the same, but inside I had changed completely. I could see that a new Elizabeth was beginning to emerge. I squeezed the crystal in my pocket.

The abbey was absolutely packed. The service was being held for the relatives of those who had died, and also for the people who had supported them – the Emergency Services, representatives of the New York Police Department, the New York Fire Department and the Family Liaison Officers. We were sitting directly below the pulpit and I could see all the television cameras. This was how my life was at the moment: I was being watched – by the cameras, the world, my family and friends, everyone waiting to see how I was going to react. Everyone, that is, except my son. My beautiful baby simply responded to my love and accepted me for whoever I was.

I looked across to where the dignitaries were sitting and saw Tony and Cherie Blair, George Bush Senior, Douglas Hurd, David Blunkett and Ken Livingstone. The hum of conversation was suddenly stilled as music began, and in walked the Queen, Prince Philip and Prince Charles. A strange thought floated through my mind. If Simon had known he was going to die he might well have chosen to do it the way he had. He had tested his courage to its ultimate degree, had been part of an event that rocked the world, and was now being remembered in a memorial service in Westminster Abbey attended by the world's dignitaries and even the Queen. It was everything he enjoyed, and he would have been so impressed. He would have loved all the pomp and circumstance that went with it. This thought really helped me in the service.

I'm an emotional person who cries at most things, even once shedding a tear during the film *Honey, I Shrunk the Kids*! But I really didn't want to cry that day. It was important to be strong for Simon and prove something to myself about my own courage. In the end it was the music that did it. We stood for the National Anthem and I cried. The first hymn was 'Dear Lord and Father of Mankind', my favourite as a child and one that Simon and I had chosen for our wedding. Of course, I cried again. During every other hymn or piece of music I put my head down and let the tears slip quietly down my face. All the way through I clasped the crystal in my pocket and worked on my visualization of the man with the cloak, trying to imagine him standing with me. I began to notice that even as I cried there was a strength running through me I hadn't felt before. Could the Reiki healing actually be working?

There was a quiet moment and into it came the sound of sobbing. It grew, and I could feel my family and friends all bending and turning with concern and sympathy, to see if there was anything they could do. Even I had to check that it wasn't me, but realized I was feeling a rush of strength from my visualization and actually felt quite calm and peaceful. It made everyone giggle for a moment with relief that I was holding it together. They had all braced themselves to support me in case the service proved too much. I was even able to walk down the aisle with Simon's stepfather to place a single rose on the memorial to terrorist victims at the front of the church. I thought of Simon and how proud he would have been and felt the strength surge through me as I held my head up. I was so proud I'd managed to do it.

From November to February, the tenor of life changed. Christmas had been and gone and time began to return to more normal dimensions. Everything had been leading up to William's birth and the memorial service and it suddenly dawned on me that I was exhausted. I had held myself together somehow for three months, and now I could stop.

In January the Red Cross contacted me to ask how best the funds they had collected and allocated to me could be used. I explained that my mother was very ill with Dad as her full-time carer, and that all my other relations lived in the North. I was on my own in London and Jan had been more than a godsend. They very kindly agreed to pay to extend her stay with me for up to a year. I was on maternity leave and didn't need to be anywhere or do anything so I chose to devote this time to recouping physically and working with her.

I also really wanted to create as much of a stable, warm, loving family home for William as I could. So life fell into a routine of bottles, naps and walks with a pram, and in between I slept and talked to Jan.

'What's the matter with you?' Jan asked one morning.

'I always wanted to have more children,' I sighed, 'and I've just realized that it may not happen for me.'

'It may or may not happen,' Jan replied, 'but make sure you don't spend your life looking for things that will make you happy, and forget the things you do have.' She sat next to me and held my hands, looking directly into my face. 'Elizabeth, some people never experience having a healthy baby boy and the joy of their own child,' she said gently.

I immediately recognized that my world had become conditional – If I was still married . . . If I had more children . . . If I had a family around me . . . If, if, if. Suddenly I looked at things differently. I was alive and had a beautiful, healthy son. I had brothers and sisters who dropped everything for me; even strangers had sent their love and support when I was at my lowest. In that simple moment Jan introduced me to the importance of acceptance and perspective. She helped me to see that living in the present would free me to enjoy my life and not be depressed about what I didn't have. I had been introduced to the holistic approach for beginners and I trusted my intuition enough now to know that my search had ended.

After that first Reiki session I began to have regular ones each week, as well as aromatherapy massage for relaxation. In the beginning the sessions were no more than gentle and relaxing but I chose to continue with them because for the first time since Simon's death I had found a way to stop the terrifying and incessant noise in my head. For an hour I was able to disappear into a sanctuary of peace. I walked into the room Jan had prepared and there was quiet music in the background, the scent of aromatherapy oils and a couch for me to lie on, and I was covered with a warm, soft blanket. All the responsibilities I carried with me from 11 September were packed away – William, grief, finances, police visits and all the other arrangements and questions that filled my head. I lay on the couch, my brain switched off and I floated in a space that required no response from me. I just felt: sadness, tears, yearning for Simon. I felt the deepest pain of loss, but I didn't try to do anything about it.

There was no talking. This was massively significant. Finding words to try to articulate how I felt was completely exhausting. For the first time, Reiki gave me the opportunity simply to feel my experience without having to explain it.

Each session was completely different. I learnt to go into each one with no expectations. There were different sensations and responses all through my body. Around my head, it was noisy and confused like a crowd of people. At my throat it was fiery, hot and restricted. My shoulders were impenetrable blocks of concrete. I could also see colours and the shapes of things but they were nearly always different from one session to another. I was aware of Jan's movements and yet I was so relaxed that I couldn't move. Every time she placed her hands in the energy centre near my stomach my emotions were released and I cried from the bottom of my soul. It was wrenching crying and yet the minute she moved away I stopped. I knew I wasn't trying to force something because I found it far easier to disregard things that weren't working. It was simply a feeling of 'this is it for me' – being in the emotion in its purest form and not having to fix it or move on from it.

I was always exhausted after a session. The combination of crying, relaxing and letting go, coupled with feelings of safety and not being judged, was exhilarating and petrifying. I slept, ironically, like a dead person after each one.

Afterwards Jan and I talked about the session and what had come up. She never told me what to think, merely allowing me to interpret what I had felt and experienced. I began to sense that although I was dealing with the grief of Simon's death, my reaction to it was predominantly shaped by who I was. The problem was that I didn't know how to react because my experience of 11 September had destroyed my values, beliefs and identity. I had many big questions about myself – Who was I? Why did I do what I did? What did I value and believe in? Who were my friends? What did love look like to me and how did I want to deal with things in life? When the Twin Towers collapsed I had also collapsed and I had to rebuild myself. I had to pick through all the debris and look at what I wanted to keep from before Simon's death and what I wanted to re-create after it. I was slowly but surely finding the inner peace and strength to start walking properly through the grief and getting braver about facing it full on. It was a huge undertaking but there was power in realizing that the choice was there.

Chapter Nine

On a daily basis my thoughts rushed back to Simon standing on the top floor of the World Trade Center with all the other people and knowing that there was fire and smoke all around them. I was terrified when I thought about how Simon must have felt. Did he know he was going to die? Was he scared? Was he one of the people that jumped? I couldn't bear to think that he might have been faced with such an obscene choice — that somehow the decision to jump from the top of the tower was better than what would happen if he stayed inside.

'Do you think Simon would have jumped?' I asked friends.

'He wasn't that type of person,' they replied.

'You will never know,' they rationalized.

'He would have inhaled the smoke and not known what had happened,' they comforted.

'He would have died before then,' they reassured.

I listened to all the explanations and knew that my friends were being kind and trying to make the situation easier for me. But my fear kept coming back. I didn't know how to accept any of the explanations and move on from this thought.

My mind came back over and over again to Simon in that place at that moment. If he didn't jump, did he have to watch other people making that choice in front of him? I wanted to believe that he had inhaled a lot of smoke and died as though he'd fallen asleep, but my inner self wouldn't accept this answer. It was like playing a game with a dog. The further I threw the ball of fear away the more enthusiastically the dog brought it right back to my feet. I knew I was playing the useless 'what if' game again, but I couldn't shake it and it was beginning to consume me.

One night Jan and I prepared for a Reiki session as normal.

'Tonight, Elizabeth,' she said, 'all you need to know is that the time is right to face your fear about Simon's death. All you have talked about is what he felt and what he went through and nothing seems to satisfy your questioning. I will hold your energy and keep you completely safe and all you need to do is go as deep as you can into the heart of your fear.'

I stared at Jan. I knew that I wouldn't settle until I did this but I was terrified of coming face to face with my deepest fear.

'What if it doesn't work?' I asked quietly.

'Well, you have to trust that you created this opportunity for yourself for a reason and if it doesn't work it's only because it will take you somewhere that will.'

I felt sick but I knew I had to do this. I had to make my choice. Go into the fear and confront it or live with it every day.

I closed my eyes and let Jan gently talk me through the process of letting go of my mind, body and spirit and connecting with my inner emotions. I knew what I had to do.

'Breathe into it, breathe into it, breathe . . .' Jan repeated as she faded away to the edge of my consciousness. I felt the warmth of the blanket, the musky smells from the oils and candles and the hardness of the couch beneath me disappear from my senses. I could see an image appearing around me. It was familiar and yet I was anxious and I panicked as I realized where I was in my meditative state. I was standing in the Windows on the World restaurant with my toes touching the floor-to-ceiling windows as I looked down at Manhattan below me. It was the position I'd been in with Simon in February 2000 when we had a drink there. I couldn't breathe as I knew what was coming.

'Breathe into it as far as you can go,' Jan whispered. 'Reach down as far as you dare and remember I'm holding your energy and I won't let anything happen to you. I will just hold you.'

I took a deep breath and allowed myself to trust as I never had before, and then it happened. I could feel Simon in the World Trade Center. I couldn't see him but I knew where I was and I knew I was feeling his energy. I felt his fear. The cold, steel-like fear that slices through your body and leaves an icy trail behind it. His whole body was wracked with terror. I felt desperation, frustration, devastation.

'Go deeper,' Jan repeated.

I pushed myself into the abyss and swam down into the darkest recesses of the trench – the trench I'd looked at before but hadn't dared to dive into in case I never came back.

I swam right to the bottom where the pitch black engulfed me and the sharp points of the bottom scraped and cut me. I was in the pit of my emotion. I knew at that point that Simon was petrified and his terror reached to the corners of his soul. Words, once again, were inadequate to describe how he felt.

I gulped for air and sobbed and sobbed. My stomach was the opening to my soul and the sobs came from the depths of this hollow space. Its emptiness was a physical pain. I panicked. I was lost in the dark and I knew it was taking me down further. I tried to grab at the sides of the abyss but it pushed me away. I felt my torment and Simon's anguish and at that moment I found his hand and he grabbed me. He held me and we were together again. Somehow in the midst of our darkest terror we had found each other. It didn't matter what had happened or where we were – I realized then that I could find Simon whenever I needed to. At the moment of facing the deepest part of our fear I felt love, I touched love, and it held me, protected me and saved me.

When Simon was in the World Trade Center on 11 September his fear was indescribable. But now I could see that he had been through that horror and his fear had ended. I realized that I was still projecting his fear onto myself but now I could stop doing that.

I felt Simon's energy leaving me in the dark but this time I knew I wasn't alone. That was a turning point when I truly felt that love was greater than everything. Simon had found me at my darkest time, Jan had held my energy so that he and I could connect, and I had found the ultimate truth deep within me. Love is at the core of us and it is as simple as that. It connects us.

Jan gently talked me back into the room.

'You were so brave. I am so proud of you.' She held me and the emotion poured out of me: the release of fear, the connection with Simon, the feeling of unconditional love, the walking through darkness and the touching of light on the other side. I cried and I cried and I cried.

After that session my grief was never as bad as it had been before. I had reached the bottom. I had opened a door and everything was able to come out and I stopped being so fearful. I had started the slow climb out of the trench.

*   *   *

At the beginning of February Jan went on holiday for two weeks and left me to fend for myself. It really did feel like that, too. I was terrified I wouldn't be able to cope but Jan knew I'd demonstrated to her that I could. The only person who didn't know that was me. She was showing me that I wasn't dependent on anyone and that I was more than capable of looking after William.

Just before Jan left I asked her if I could complete my Reiki 1 Attunement. This level is all about practising Reiki on yourself and working on your own issues. I was loving what Reiki had done for me so far and knew that it had given me courage and strength now that I had access to all the tools that I held within me.

I now understood that my life was my own responsibility and that blame and anger were not a way forward. My anger would never hurt the terrorists, it would only hurt me. The choices I made were helping me create the life that I wanted after Simon's death and my intuition, trust and emotion were all tools in the process of learning to walk again. Jan was continually encouraging my independence.

This prepared me well for Jan's time away. I did Reiki on myself every day and structured my time carefully. I knew that if I managed my own well-being, then by default William would be looked after.

It was during this time that we all came to a decision about a proper funeral. I had thought that perhaps something might have been identified of Simon, as many of his colleagues had been found. But five months on all I had was a pristine Virgin flying card, literally without a mark on it. So with no body and receding hope that there would ever be one, we decided to go ahead with a private service of memorial instead.

The night before the service, my dad came down to stay. This was a huge emotional mountain to face because I hadn't seen either of my parents since Simon had been killed. I understood the reasons for that: Dad had had to make a decision to look after Mum or me and no parent would find that choice easy.

'You have your brother and sisters down there looking after you,' Dad had said, 'whereas your mum has no one but me.'

I had listened to it all and I absorbed it but I really struggled with it – not as an adult but as a small child. I had found it very difficult to accept that in the most testing time of my life my dad hadn't come to be with me.

I was angry, sad, confused and hurt. I felt all these things not because I thought that as parents they should have been with me but because I had wanted them there more than anyone in the world. I needed my mum and dad. They had been tremendously loving as I grew up and I needed that tangible love now as well as their words of wisdom and for them to make it all right. If ever there was a point in my life that I truly became an adult it was then. I couldn't have asked for better stand-ins than Catherine, Ron, Mark and Deborah, but that was the moment when I learnt the lesson of self-responsibility.

I also felt deeply hurt for me and sad for William that three months after my son was born, my parents hadn't met him. I needed other people to show that they loved William as much as I did and above all I needed that from my parents. My anger and sadness grew every day and I knew that they were harming me more than anyone else.

So I was nervous when Dad came to stay. I opened the door and felt a huge ball of emotional energy between us. There were so many unsaid feelings, words and emotions. How on earth were we going to deal with this in time for the service the next day?

I wanted and needed to say how it had all felt as I couldn't afford to take it with me to Simon's memorial service. I was angry and I wanted to shout about it but Dad isn't a shouting man and we both knew that choosing that childlike approach wouldn't help either of us. I have learnt never to underestimate my dad's wisdom. He knew exactly what we had to deal with that night and I respected him for allowing me the space to say what I needed to.

I told him that I felt hurt and let down, that I had wanted them both to be with me and was confused by their response to this need, and how I couldn't understand why it seemed like a big request from me.

That night my dad began to explain the choices he had made and he also said one thing that ultimately began to rebuild the bridge between us.

'Elizabeth, there'll come a point in your life with William where you'll have to make a difficult decision about how to handle him. I've had to make that decision and it was whether to be with your mum or with you. I searched deeply to work out what to do and I chose to be with your mum because you could be with your brother and sisters. The moment arrives where you have to trust that you've equipped your children to be adults so that whatever life throws at them, they have the tools, skills and knowledge to find their way through without their parents to hold them up. Quite simply, your mum needed me more.'

I listened and I understood, but I wasn't quite ready at that point to accept these words. Dad was telling me his truth, that this decision created many ripple effects that affected many different people. It hadn't been easy for him and it wasn't my place to judge it. I had a choice now too, and that was whether or not to stop being angry with Dad. It would take time, but I knew that enough love and forgiveness were there for it to happen. Taking our time would be fine. I felt I'd suddenly become an adult and not the youngest child any more. I knew I'd be a better mum to William by facing the realities and choices of being a parent.

The next morning was 22 February: 22.02.2002. It looked like a significant date to have chosen to remember Simon. This service was only about Simon and I thought it would be the hardest one. It had to reflect everything Simon was and stood for.

I also had to be everything Simon loved me for. I needed to be strong and to make him proud of the way I dealt with the service, his friends and the whole day. I could feel the pressure mounting and escaped to the sanctuary of my bedroom for a few moments of peace to prepare for the day ahead.

I sat on my bed and closed my eyes. I visualized a beam of light which was connected to the universal energy around us and came down into the top of my head, going all the way through the middle of my body and right down into the earth below me. The beam of light carried on to the centre of the earth and anchored itself there. I was connected to the universe and I was anchored to the earth. I then imagined a beautiful rainbow-coloured bubble encircling me to protect me and my energy from the huge level of emotion that would be present during the day. I saw a pond in my stomach with clear spring water. I felt the serenity and stillness of that pond and recognized that during the day I could come back to it whenever I felt that I was losing my centre. I took a deep breath and I knew that I was ready to say goodbye to Simon.

I walked into the church holding William and saw that it was completely full. There were galleries higher up and even they were packed too. Every seat was taken up by friends and family who had come to say goodbye to Simon. The HAC padre, Reverend David Reindorp, took the service. He and Simon had been friends so he understood the essence of Simon and couldn't have been a better man for the job. But just as David began, William decided that he wanted his presence known and he screamed and screamed. As David waited for him to stop, I couldn't help thinking how appropriate it was for William to make his mark like that.

David began by telling us how he was certain that Simon would have passed over and then immediately organized a cocktail party so that everyone could meet and get to know each other despite the horrendous circumstances of their death. Laughter echoed around the church, and I knew that it all felt right. Simon would have loved us laughing.

The address that Pete gave for Simon would have made him laugh too, and cry, smile, squirm and value him as a friend even more. He acknowledged the huge gap that Simon's death had left in our lives, and why we loved him the way he was – sociable, dedicated, loyal and sensitive; a lover of good food and wine – and the occasional cigar; a pedantic perfectionist . . .

'I remember going to his flat once in south London,' Pete said, 'and there was an indexing system for the herbs and spices, and a wine-rotating list to ensure the sediment never got too thick, although this was hardly ever used because of the socializing that Simon enjoyed so much!'

Pete described how Simon's love for me had made him whole, and what a wonderful father he would have been. He was eternally sad that Simon had missed that, but grateful for the privilege of his friendship. Finally, Pete described his faith in his best friend and his certain knowledge in how Simon would have faced the event that killed him.

'Even if he knew what was going to happen that morning, Simon's dominant qualities would have shone through to the last: his compassion for others and sense of service.

'He would have helped people trying to get out, he would have made sure the room was clear of everyone he was responsible for, he would have tried to calm others, he would have tried to organize help.'

Pete knew Simon so well and his words made the service even more perfect.

I was beginning to learn at these events that the music always floored me and my family. Even some of the male contingent couldn't maintain their composure when Simon's favourite hymns, 'Jerusalem' and 'I Vow to Thee my Country', were sung. Once again, I lowered my head, let the tears fall and took myself back to the calm pond in my centre, pulling strength from its deep stillness. I didn't feel helpless in my grief now. I still had to deal with it and face it but the lessons I had learnt, the Reiki and my knowledge of a bigger picture, meant that I was accepting my emotions and my journey from sadness, and was now choosing to flow with them. I wasn't trying to fight them any more. I felt strong and peaceful holding our son at Simon's service.

The day was a really good reflection of the man Simon was and I knew he was proud. It was perfect in every way except that he couldn't be with us. I was proud of myself too as I'd been given the opportunity to test how I was dealing with my grief on one of the most emotionally difficult days. I realized that my choices were giving me my power back. I was able to prepare myself internally for a day of huge emotion and had managed to keep my centre strong and calm. The route I'd chosen had given me the one thing I was looking for: peace.

Peace. It does not mean to be in a place where there is no noise, trouble or hard work. It means to be in the midst of those things and still be calm in your heart.

Chapter Ten

It was almost six months to the day when I was finally able to make the journey to Manhattan to see where my husband had died. I had decided to travel with Celine – one of Simon's best friends and one of William's godmothers. She is such a strong, independent woman, and I knew why Simon loved her so much. They had a huge connection and I felt that some of it had transferred to me following Simon's death. It would be an important journey for her too, because she had been due to fly out with Simon for the conference. At the last minute she'd had to change her plans and stayed in London.

As we pulled out of the Lincoln Tunnel Celine and I quickly looked down towards the end of Manhattan, waiting to see the huge gap in the skyline where the World Trade Center had previously stood defiantly in the sky. That night, a thick fog lay over the whole of the island and we couldn't see a thing. In remembrance of the six-month anniversary the city of New York had installed two massive lights that faced up to the sky, ethereal versions of the Twin Towers. I imagined them being like ghosts, as Simon was. But that night wasn't the moment for us to see any of this, and we quietly made our way into Manhattan. The whole city tasted, smelt and felt like Simon and it was strange to be there after thinking about it for six months.

I kept expecting him to appear. I was scared. What horrors, fears and nightmares would this journey bring up? Or would it be healing and nourishing and help me to move forward?

When I woke up the next morning I felt sick again. The apprehension of what lay ahead was already there. It was a Tuesday morning and I'd arrived in Manhattan late on Monday night, just like Simon. I felt as though I were following in his footsteps. In the morning he'd phoned me just after having his shower and before he went to the World Trade Center, and I found I was doing exactly the same thing. I woke up and showered and then I phoned Jan to speak to William before I started to make my way to Ground Zero. Even with all the shocks I had already encountered since September the similarity of the day still stopped me in my tracks. I ran over to the window to see what the sky looked like. I was hoping that it would be thick fog like the night before, but instead it was a vivid blue without a single cloud.

A clothing ritual was developing as each event took place. I got dressed in a pair of trousers, a top and a jacket that Simon had told me he liked. I also chose a big black coat he loved. I'd worn it to both his memorial services and it seemed appropriate therefore to be wearing it to his real grave. Simon told me that I looked as though I'd stepped out of the Scottish Widows advert, the irony of which was clearly not lost on anyone when I wore it to Ground Zero.

Once dressed, I thought about what jewellery I wanted to wear. My wedding ring was important, but it had never carried as much sentimental value as my engagement ring. Simon told me how he'd visited one of the Jewish dealers in the diamond district on a business trip to New York, and chosen the diamond he wanted to use. He then designed the setting with the jeweller and followed the diamond around the workshop while the ring was made. It was exquisite, but there was much more to it than that. Simon had put so much of who he was and what he thought of me into the ring, and it therefore felt like more of a representation of our relationship than anything else. When he gave it to me, I laughed with him, saying that I'd have to go through labour before he gave me any more diamonds. But Simon didn't work like that. He gave me some beautiful diamond earrings for our wedding and a diamond pendant necklace to mark the beginning of the new millennium. Each piece was subtle and quiet, but they held Simon's love for me and were hugely important. In what felt a little like a ceremony, I put them all on for my visit to Ground Zero.

First, we had to go to the British Consulate to meet a representative who would tell us about Ground Zero and answer any questions. I had a bad taste in my mouth because Consulate rules and regulations had nearly prevented Amanda, my Family Liaison Officer, from coming with me to New York. As I was travelling six months after the event some of the arrangements had been altered and it was now the rule that British families would be accompanied by someone from the Consulate. That was fine if the families had already visited the site but as I had been pregnant and William was only small I felt that I should be able to have my Family Liaison Officer with me. The Consulate had told us that this was impossible. My family were concerned that although I was going with Celine, we were both visiting Ground Zero for the first time and both of us were vulnerable. I was incensed by the need for rules and regulations in a situation as sensitive as this. I didn't want to be with a stranger on this journey. I desperately needed to feel that the people around me knew me, cared for me and were protecting me. I needed Amanda to be there and I wasn't about to let some unconnected official tell me how I was going to visit my husband's place of death.

Amanda's boss, DI Osborn, had worked hard on my behalf to explain my situation to the relevant superiors. He outlined the important role that Amanda had played with my family since we all found ourselves involved in the events of 11 September 2001. He told them how exceptional I thought Amanda was at her job and how vital it was that I had the reassurance of her presence in New York, where I didn't have direct access to my family and was having to take one of the most difficult journeys of my life. DI Osborn somehow managed to get the decision overruled and Amanda came with me to New York.

So we gathered at the Consulate and the pleasantries began with their staff.

'My trip is going well so far,' I said, 'especially because I have Amanda, my Family Liaison Officer, with me. It's lovely to have someone who knows me so well, so that if anything happens my family knows that either Amanda will look after me or she'll contact them straight away.'

I knew I was being childish and underlining an issue but I couldn't help myself. Anyway I'd made my point and was prepared to leave the situation alone and give these people the opportunity to make up lost ground. However, that wasn't to be the case. I began to talk to Celine about William and one of the staff asked me who William was.

'William is my son,' I explained.

'Oh, I'm sorry. I didn't realize,' he replied.

I was astounded. I would have understood if I'd come over

in the immediate aftermath of the attacks and information hadn't been put together on the families or even the people who had died, but this was six months on and I was the only British family member visiting Ground Zero at that time. I just wanted to leave and go to the site and be on my own.

I got outside as quickly as I could and tried to breathe in the blue sky again. I was beginning to feel claustrophobic. We climbed into the car and waited to begin our journey. I was quiet, and Amanda leant over and asked gently if I was all right. I nodded, but as I looked at her I saw a row of flags hanging on a building behind her. I don't know why they caught my attention, but my instinct drew me to look more closely. It was an unremarkable hotel, but it looked familiar. I searched the façade for something that might identify it.

'What are you staring at? Amanda asked.

I went absolutely silent.

'Elizabeth, what's the matter?' She was starting to look concerned.

'Celine,' I said. 'Look at that hotel.' She turned round and went quiet.

The car was parked right outside the Pickwick Arms, the hotel Simon had stayed in the night before he went to the conference at the World Trade Center. The coincidences I'd experienced since Simon's death were becoming regular and noticeable. Indeed, I was finding it hard to believe they *were* simply coincidences, but I didn't have any other explanation for them. Finding myself outside Simon's hotel was incredible. I was now going to make a journey identical to his on the morning he died.

We stopped briefly at Simon's old offices and picked up a beautiful bouquet of white lilies to take with us. There was also a wonderful picture of Simon that the staff had laminated for me. It was taken on our honeymoon and he had a big wide smile on his face. He looked tanned, happy and in a wonderful place in his life, and he was holding a bottle of champagne and two glasses. I wanted a picture at Ground Zero that showed the essence of Simon and this was definitely it. I had added a message at the bottom from William and me and it represented the past, present and future. It was a message about 11 September and then a message to Simon. I was going to place it at his official grave; it had to be just right.

Simon James Turner
17.7.62

Peace
It does not mean to be in a place
Where there is no noise, trouble or hard work
It means to be in the midst of those things
and still be calm in your heart
•
I stood on tip toe gazing into the distance
interminably gazing at the road that had taken you...

We miss you
Elizabeth Turner, Wife
William Turner, Son
born 14.11.01

I had seen the Twin Towers many times but I couldn't imagine them now and even when we turned the corner and saw the space where they'd stood I couldn't remember how high they'd been or how much they'd dominated the area. Celine was shaken by the hole in the city. She had worked in the World Trade Center many times and was clearly very shocked by how much space there was in the absence of the buildings. We were all quiet as we walked through the barriers. I didn't know what to expect or what to feel.

We walked along a wooden gangway that took us to the family viewing centre. All the way down the right-hand side was a rough, makeshift plywood fence. It was the kind of wood you normally see boarding up a broken window or shop front and it had a temporary feel to it. In contrast to this was the white sign running the length of the fence which served as a memorial to 11 September 2001. There was a large image of the head of the Statue of Liberty and then a list of all the names of the people who had died including those who had been on American Airlines Flight 11 and United Airlines Flight 175.

The list seemed to go on forever, column after column after column, all the names in alphabetical order like a school class register announcing the attendance of all these people on the day of their death. So many people killed in a few short hours: families bereaved; children without parents; parents without children. People without a choice whether or not they died that day, who never had a chance to say goodbye. Lists and lists of the consequence of other people trying to exercise their right to a viewpoint. I felt a deep sadness at Simon's grave and a sense of denial at his death being presented in such a weird, huge and public way. I felt very insignificant.

Across the top of the white board

capital letters. 'I pray that our heave

anguish of your bereavement, and le

memory of the loved and lost, and t

be yours to have laid so costly a s

freedom.' (Abraham Lincoln)

I read the saying and then I read i

it registered completely. The poigna

words to explain something where w

but I hated the phrase 'to have laid

the altar of freedom'. I could hear t

'But we weren't at war! Simon went

I thought of our trips to Normandy

curious Simon had been about cou

war. Perhaps I shouldn't be so ang

whole event have confused some p

angry but I hadn't felt anger towa

they did. I don't know why, it was

ways their actions remained uncon

with and the pain of my experienc

knew that anger and hatred only

violence.

I continued walking around the

all it was: a plywood stage from wh

that was once the World Trade

dump trucks, cranes and workmen.

to see in a construction site. Mud, di

and red netting around unsafe ar

before I came to New York that the

affected by their work within Grou

124

established their own respectful rituals whenever they found something vital. Despite the noise of the site I felt a deep sense of peace there. I leant against the barrier in silence for a long time, staring at the work going on. The sky was still a glorious deep blue and the day was very warm. I took my black coat off.

All available space on the plywood walls was taken up by displays. Pictures of smiling faces, flowers, wreaths, photographs, posters, letters, birthday cards, Christmas cards, messages, American flags and a host of little angels painted by children. On the one hand I felt insignificant as Simon had died with so many people and yet on another I was beginning to realize for the first time the enormity of the event in which he'd died.

For the past six months I hadn't really connected with the reality around me. As I stood at Ground Zero I felt a part of me responding to the experience. I had come out of the protection I'd created around myself and William in London and instead of being a wife, a pregnant woman or a new mother I was standing there being Elizabeth. For the first time in a long time – since I fell pregnant in February, even – everything around me was about Elizabeth and not the baby or Simon.

I stood for such an age that I lost track of time. I felt very close to Simon at Ground Zero but being there also made me realize that he was dead and gone. He wouldn't be part of my life any more and there was nothing I could do to get him back. I thought about Simon knowing he was about to die, and I hoped deeply that in that moment he was able to say that he'd lived his life the way he'd truly wanted to. I will never know whether he did or not but I knew then that on the day I died I needed to be able to say it to myself. I wanted my life to be the best it could be – to be able to say that I was true to myself and my life's experiences.

'What does happen next?' I asked myself quietly. I wondered how on earth I was going to get on the tube in London and go back to work.

Then I began to feel something else. The enormity of my experience really hit me. I couldn't change what had happened to me on 11 September 2001 as I had no control over those events, but I did have control over how I reacted to them. What happened next was my responsibility. I didn't know how I was going to do it but I instinctively knew there was no way I could ever return to the life I'd had before. The landscape had changed. My situation was completely different but I was also thinking differently about my life and how to live it.

I think that was the moment my new life truly began, as I could see I had a choice. Everything was beginning to make sense. It was my choice now whether to try to re-create the normality I had before or to embrace the extraordinary nature of my situation. Instinctively I felt the pull towards the extraordinary.

I realized that my time with William was the greatest gift I had been given and I should not squander it. I understood that eventually he would move on and that life was so short I should spend it only doing things I was passionate about. So I made a decision not to return to corporate life and promised myself I would leave a footprint with my life that had a positive impact and made a positive change – not only for me but for William.

I was exhausted when I got back to the hotel after the visit. I thought we'd only been at Ground Zero for half an hour, but in fact we'd been there nearly three hours. Later that night I went out for a walk, hoping to digest the day's events and my thoughts.

I didn't really know where I was going but it didn't matter. I saw a couple walking towards me, hand in hand. They smiled, hugged and kissed each other, oblivious to everyone else in the world. As they walked past, the reality of my never having that with Simon again hit me. He was never coming back. The emotion from the day was unplugged and I gulped as the sadness, fear, shock and trauma of the last six months poured out of me. I walked and walked, sobbing the whole way, and thought where better to let the emotion flow out but the city in which Simon had been taken from me.

I found myself exhausted, red-eyed and washed out at the Rockefeller Center. There is a centrepiece with the words of Rockefeller etched into it and as I came to the end of my emotional fallout I found myself standing in front of them.

I believe in the supreme worth of the individual and in his right to life, liberty and the pursuit of happiness.

I believe that every right implies a responsibility; every opportunity, an obligation; every possession, a duty.

I believe that the law was made for man and not man for the law; that government is the servant of the people and not their master.

I believe in the dignity of labor, whether with head or hand; that the world owes no man a living but that it owes every man an opportunity to make a living.

I believe that thrift is essential to well ordered living and that economy is a prime requisite of a sound financial structure, whether in government, business or personal affairs.

I believe that truth and justice are fundamental to an enduring social order.

I believe in the sacredness of a promise, that a man's word should be as good as his bond; that character — not wealth or power or position — is of supreme worth.

I believe that the rendering of useful service is the common duty of mankind and that only in the purifying fire of sacrifice is the dross of selfishness consumed and the greatness of the human soul set free.

I believe in an all-wise and all-loving God, named by whatever name, and that the individual's highest fulfilment, greatest happiness, and widest usefulness are to be found in living in harmony with His will.

I believe that love is the greatest thing in the world; that it alone can overcome hate; that right can and will triumph over might.

The words were all about the choices we can make as individuals and they reinforced the decision I'd made while standing at Ground Zero that day. A lot of lessons were falling into place.

*   *   *

The next day Celine and I visited Simon's offices in SoHo. Many of the people there had either watched the event, were supposed to have been at the World Trade Center or knew of other people who had been killed on the day. They had suffered tremendous grief and loss yet they'd still thought to buy me flowers and put them in the office I was going to be in all day so that I could meet everyone. I knew it was going to be a hard day, but what I didn't expect was how amazing it was to be with other people whose lives had been changed by 11 September 2001 and to share the tragic experience with such love, generosity and compassion.

The stories of the day began. One girl told me she'd been stuck in the subway; another colleague described how his friend had been caught in the fireball that came out of the lift; and another about the man who had four sons, three of whom joined the fire brigade while he'd managed to convince the last one to become a trader at Cantor Fitzgerald. Another colleague told me he'd chosen to work at Risk Waters because of Simon.

One of the team had been to the top of the World Trade Center to deliver some magazines but Simon had asked for some Waters magazines as well and sent him back to the office to pick them up before the conference started. On his way back he saw a sick bird and spent some time looking after it and finding a safe place for it. He watched the whole thing unfold with the planes and the buildings collapsing. This colleague was the last person to see everyone at the conference alive.

So many people shared their stories with me and it all helped to build a picture of what New Yorkers had had to deal with on that day and what they were all still clearly dealing with. They were frightened and hurting, yet a huge degree of friendship, care and concern was displayed by everyone I came across. I had never experienced these types of connection on any other trip I'd made to the city. Despite the trauma I preferred the city that I was part of now, and it helped me recognize the significant effects of the event in which I had been involved and to shift my perspective on Simon's death.

That evening, we drove down to Ground Zero where we saw the Towers of Light for the first time. They tipped upward, two huge blue lights, whose beams stretched from the ground up into heaven, where they dissolved into the clouds. They were indeed ghostly. It seemed as though for one night the Towers had returned, like the story of Brigadoon, the spectral village that appeared every hundred years. Mum and I used to watch that film, and she loved the idea that the village disappeared magically back into the clouds. I thought the connection between the film and the Towers of Light was a beautiful memorial to remember the people who had died there.

Ground Zero at night felt very peaceful despite all the work that was going on and I was really pleased that we had gone down again. It was so special to see Simon's face staring out and smiling with his champagne. It felt right, as though he had a resting place there. No longer was he a name or number but a person smiling out to everyone.

As I'd been at the site the day before I was able to feel more relaxed and breathe there this time. I was in such turmoil when I first visited that I didn't find my space within it and by returning at night when it was dark and quieter it felt much more personal and connected.

There were a few people around looking at the pictures and messages. I noticed one man and a younger woman who didn't appear to be reading anything and I found myself watching them to see what they were doing. I noticed that they were carrying little boxes full of pins.

'What are you doing?' I asked.

'We're just going round putting extra pins into all the messages and posters so they don't fall down,' the older man said. 'This is my daughter and we like to do this whenever we can.'

It was the simplest act and yet the impact of their thoughtfulness was enormous.

Celine and I talked towards the end of our trip about everything that had happened and she wanted to know what I had come away with, having seen Ground Zero. There were many things. I knew I had reconnected with myself and the world and that I was now aware of the choices I had in front of me. I had faced my grief over Simon and it was time to decide who I would become after the past six months. Did I want to accept that this was done to me and there was nothing I could do, or did I want to take responsibility for my own experience? Did I want to find my own way through this or expect others to do it for me? I remembered the two people pinning up posters and it reminded me of all the kindness I had seen since Simon had died. Out of such a horrific event the world had also demonstrated enormous love and compassion. Did I want to choose love or hate? I knew that no one should ever have to feel pain at this level and so my only choice was to break the cycle. I had to stop the anger. Vengeance of any kind could never be the answer.

Finally, I told her that in the first days after 11 September I would have given up being pregnant to have Simon back. But

I now realized that I didn't want or need to trade. William was part of Simon and me and even though I loved Simon with all my heart, William was my priority. I was on a new path and I was joined by William. I knew Simon would agree. Something about this trip to New York had moved and changed and clicked within me, and it was a good thing. I was grateful to be sharing this with Celine. I suddenly felt my own power being reignited. I had a long way to go but I knew I had choices and they were liberating.

It was our last night in New York and we took a taxi down to Ground Zero for the last time. We looked at the Towers of Light and they were covered in mist and rain again. Just like Brigadoon, New York disappeared from my life and I knew I would only return when I needed to visit it again. I also now knew that Simon was with me and he was coming home with me in my heart.

Chapter Eleven

When I returned from New York I felt as though I had woken from my grief and stepped back into the world. I wasn't doing much more than simply standing up, but I was doing that and I was aware of what was going on around me. I realized that my life had changed, that I had changed, and that I felt much more connected to Simon. I lost him on 11 September but I had reconnected with his presence and it was wonderfully reassuring.

It probably didn't make sense to anyone else but there were so many subtle things I noticed or felt that made me feel I wasn't on my own. Whether they had always been there or whether I was more aware of them now that the shock was beginning to lift, I don't know. I noticed that light bulbs blew when I needed Simon near. Certain songs that were special to us came on the radio when I thought of him and I often read things that answered a question in my mind.

Each time I noticed one of them I thought how amazing and comforting it was, but then the next time it was even more noticeable. I kept asking for more confirmation and each time I did, something popped up. I began to look forward to the little signs but the one experience that made me decide to accept this situation as real was around the time I had to deal with my first wedding anniversary without Simon. I was dreading it but knew that I had to go through it whether I liked it or not. The feelings of sadness grew daily as the date approached.

It was a Monday night, which meant it was bin night. I collected all the rubbish from around the house and as I did it I thought about how normal I must look to the outside world. A new mum with a baby asleep upstairs, moving from room to room, collecting the rubbish from the waste bins. And yet my situation, my experience, my feelings and grief were anything but normal. All these thoughts went round and round my head and I wanted to have Simon near me as our anniversary approached. Just a hug, just a look, just one of his winks which said, 'I love you and I will take care of you always.' I opened the front door into the dark, wet night and carried the bags of rubbish to the bin. As I did this I looked down the garden path and parked right outside my gate was a brand-new, racing-green Mini Cooper. Simon loved Mini Coopers. They were his favourite car and consequently his favourite film was *The Italian Job*. I also knew that there was no one on my road who owned one, and I'd never seen one parked there before.

Before I met him Simon had just sold his Mini Cooper and bought a red sports car. It didn't last long in his affections and he kept talking about the fact that he preferred a Mini and wanted to sell the sports car and buy another one. I had decided it was a great opportunity, as his fortieth was coming up, to buy him one for his birthday. What he really wanted was the old-style car, and his favourite colour was red. So I'd met up in secret with Ron in London to look at the viability of buying a second-hand red Mini Cooper to give to Simon.

I stood and looked at the brand-new car outside my house

and felt a sense of disappointment. I realized that if Simon was trying to say he was with me this wasn't what he would have arranged. If he really wanted to show me he was around he would have had an old red Mini Cooper parked outside my house. I resigned myself to the fact that I was on my own.

I pulled the wheelie bin out through the gate and onto the road. I did this job every Monday night and I vividly remembered doing it on 10 September 2001. I was heavily pregnant then and Simon was in New York; this time my son was asleep upstairs and Simon was dead. He'd never pulled the bins out before he died so it was always my job, but now it felt like a burden because there was no chance of anyone other than me doing it. I was feeling very, very sad and alone that night and knowing that Simon wasn't close made it all feel worse. I went back inside and closed the door.

Just before I went to bed I picked up the last bits of rubbish from the kitchen and decided to put them outside in the bin before I locked the house up for the night. I opened the door and started walking down the path. I looked up and stopped dead in my tracks. There was still a car parked directly in front of my house but it wasn't the same one. In exactly the same place there was now an old red Mini Cooper. I felt the hairs all over my body stand up.

I was blown away by what had just happened. I looked around to see if there was anyone there but the road was completely empty. I must have looked a real sight to my neighbours, standing stock still in the street in my pyjamas and slippers with a rubbish bag in my hand, staring at a clapped-out old banger. But then I felt the joy rising up inside me and I smiled and laughed out loud. I said a silent thank you. I really felt that he had pulled it out of the bag for me just before our wedding anniversary. It was as though he'd saved his best card till last and waited for it to have the strongest impact possible, and it really did.

I walked back up my path, took one more look at the car and then closed the door. I switched on the hall light. It blew. I slept really well that night and the next morning when I looked out of my window the car was gone. I never saw it again. But I didn't need to. I had asked for the ultimate confirmation and I got it. To this day I know that Simon is always with me and William. I still see signs that he's near me but I don't need to ask for them any more.

The Mini Cooper experience also signified another change in my journey through grief. Although Simon was physically dead I began to realize that there was a way our connection could continue, and this helped me to think that I might be able to move forward on my own with the feeling that he was always with me. It was a start.

At the beginning of April 2002 I found myself joining an all-boys' HAC tour. It was a wonderful opportunity to experience something Simon had loved so much.

The HAC is the oldest unit in the British Army and was chartered by Henry VIII in 1537. For seventeen years, Simon had felt proud and honoured to be part of this Company and made many long-standing friends, including his best man, Pete Willett. While he was a part of the regiment he felt it was possible to give to two other things and for the seventeen years before I met him they had been friends and work. I fell in love with him knowing the role it played in his life and would never have asked him to leave to spend more time with me. But in 2000, just a year after we got married, Simon decided that the time had come to concentrate on his marriage, his career and, as always, his friends. He resigned as an active member but continued to enjoy the social side of the company.

Four months after Simon died the Regimental Sergeant Major, Steve Ashley, came to the house with Pete to talk to me about an idea that had been developed by a number of the members of the HAC to remember Simon and to raise money to support William's future. His friends had gone into action the moment they heard Simon had gone missing on 11 September. It didn't matter that he was no longer an active member. In their eyes he was part of the HAC family. It was incredibly moving.

The idea they'd come up with was to run two marathons over a three-day period, one in Pirbright (the army base) pulling a 2000lb field gun, and the second in Boston, home of the Ancient and Honourable Artillery Company (AHAC), the sister company of the HAC in London. The AHAC was as old, traditional and prestigious as the HAC and running the Boston Marathon was a way of demonstrating British-American solidarity. In addition both Flight 11 and Flight 175 (the two flights that were crashed into the Twin Towers) had set off from Boston and many people from this area had died on 11 September 2001. This gave the event a special poignancy.

It was an enormous challenge and it felt quite overwhelming when they explained their plan. I cried with the emotion of it.

Pete, Jan, William and I arrived at Pirbright on the day of the gun-pulling marathon, and I went straight into interview sessions with lots of TV shows and newspapers. It finally felt right to talk to the press about my experience on 11 September and William's birth, in the context of my wonderful connection with the HAC. It gave me the opportunity to show that people can decide how they react in these tragedies. We can retaliate or we can choose a path of friendship, love and resilience. I wanted to highlight the latter choice.

At Pirbright, the team bonded over the sheer physicality of the challenge as they pulled a gun the size of a small car around twenty-six miles. They were running in army boots and had to keep the gun from rolling off in different directions. The limits they pushed themselves to were incredible. All the supporters, including many of Simon's friends, the families of the team and members of the HAC, cheered them on enthusiastically as they passed by on their numerous circuits. The team completed the challenge in four hours and fifty-seven minutes. It was an extraordinary time. The champagne popped and the team celebrated in the little time they had before regrouping for the next stage of their adventure. In just over twenty-four hours they would be preparing for their second marathon and although physically they had done the hardest part of the challenge, Boston would be something else.

On the flight, I could see that the boys had developed a huge camaraderie during their time training and running together. They had helped, encouraged and supported each other. They were a band of brothers and I was the sister coming along with them. On one hand I relished the opportunity to see a part of what Simon had loved so much but on the other I struggled with his absence, and spending time with these wonderful men reminded me of what I missed so much.

As soon as we arrived we met Joe Benoit, Captain of the Ancient and Honourable Artillery Company. I immediately felt comfortable with this kind man. He was such a gentleman, a quality I found over and over again in both the HAC and the AHAC. There was a connection with Joe that I felt as soon as I met him. I couldn't explain it but I knew it was there.

On the morning of the marathon the guys were excited and the adrenalin began to pump. Once everyone had got their T-shirts on, along with their plasters, flags, rucksacks, water bottles, nipple covers, army boots and combat trousers, as well as eating a mammoth breakfast, we were ready to set off for the starting line. You would never have thought they were going to run a marathon with what they were wearing but this was what they wanted to do. They were proud and showed all the qualities you'd expect from the armed forces: integrity, respect, honour, loyalty and, most of all, determination. I couldn't imagine a better way to remember Simon, who'd demonstrated all these qualities on a daily basis.

Once again the media onslaught began but this time there was a greater feeling of fun. Steve did all the interviews with me and I felt like I was with my big brother. He kept an eye on me throughout and I felt safe. The interviewers were all intrigued by this group of soldiers and the guys revelled in their moment of fame, particularly when a number of girls advertising Hawaiian Tropic suntan oil came over to say hello!

The 106th Boston Marathon had 11 September as its moving focus. At the starting line there was a big sign which read, 'Never Forget ... Sept. 11, 2001 – Hopkinton Marathon Committee'. A lot of the runners wore the Stars and Stripes logo somewhere on their running kit and there were notices strapped to people with images of friends and family who'd died on the flights. Everyone was feeling the day.

The lads made their way to the start and Pete and I walked to the barriers so we could cheer the team on as they ran past. First to start were the disabled runners, all in their speed-designed wheelchairs, helmets and 'go faster' clothes. I was humbled, and reminded of others who'd had to face adversity and overcome their situation. I recognized the message that I too could choose to live again.

The gun was fired and the wheelchair athletes shot off into the distance. Next to start were the elite runners, followed finally by the 80 per cent of normal people running the marathon for their own personal reasons. Our team were part of that group and I felt a surge of pride as they ran past us together in perfect formation.

Everyone cheered and waved flags at them; the crowds shouted William's name and 'Go army!' wherever they were on the course. At one point they went past the Boston Girls' Wellesley College and all the girls were outside shouting and cheering for the team and handing out kisses. As they ran past a café full of Hells Angels they were amazed to hear the revving of fifty Harley Davidsons in support of what they were doing. It was deeply moving.

While we were waiting at the finish line, I was filmed by Lucy from the Films of Record camera crew who were shooting the anniversary film *September Mourning*. She took the opportunity to ask me what the marathon meant to me. Halfway through our conversation she asked, 'Do you miss William?'

I burst into tears. I was finding it very hard to be away from William and this was exacerbated by how much the HAC reminded me of Simon. By this time William was starting to develop a distinct personality and I felt the absence of him acutely. I was really beginning to feel the impact this little boy had quite rightly had on my life.

At 6 p.m. word went up that the team were coming through. Regimental Sergeant Major Steve Ashley had them all marching into the final straight, standing tall, backs straight, arms moving in unison and all looking straight ahead with absolute military pride and precision. They had completed it in five hours and fifteen minutes. Two marathons in three days wearing combats and army boots and the first pulling a two-ton gun. It was unbelievable.

I was bursting with pride that they had done all this for my little boy and in memory of Simon. No wonder he was in the HAC for seventeen years! Many of the guys didn't want to come near me in case they cried, some of them hugged me so much I could barely breathe, and all of them realized the enormity of what they had achieved. It was an incredible feeling for all of us.

That evening the AHAC hosted a dinner for the team and everyone who had supported them and made the event happen. It was held in my honour which was humbling and made me feel a little uncomfortable given that I hadn't run two marathons back to back. Captain Joe Benoit gave a speech and I was presented with a brooch of the USS *Constitution*, which is the oldest commissioned ship afloat in the world. Joe explained the history of the Boston frigate, known as 'Old Ironsides', a wooden-hulled, three-masted heavy frigate of the United States Navy, named after the United States Constitution.

I laughed. I resembled a frigate that had demonstrated longevity, an iron will and a strong constitution, and was one of the last frigates of her time still to be floating! After the last six months these comparisons felt highly appropriate. I picked the brooch out of the box and pinned it onto my coat. It was beautiful and I knew I'd treasure it as a reminder of our time in Boston.

The next day, we were all invited to the AGM of the AHAC at their headquarters to meet the members of this incredible old establishment. Up until this point, no woman had ever been present at an AHAC AGM – 300 years of history was about to change. The HAC filed to the front of the room and Joe Benoit gave a speech of thanks to everyone who had been involved. Then, to my complete surprise, he invited me up to say a few words. I'd had no idea that I was going to be asked to do this so hadn't prepared anything to say. I walked slowly towards the podium and looked around the huge oak room, feeling the eyes of all the commanding officers' portraits looking at me from down the years. This was my opportunity to say thank you. I felt the room take a deep breath with me. If ever there was a moment when Simon would be watching this was it.

I spoke from the heart about what the event had meant to me and how proud and overwhelmed I was by everyone's kindness and love for William, Simon and me. I thanked them for turning the events of 11 September into something so heartwarming and special, an achievement I'd be able to talk to William about for the rest of my life.

I don't think I took a breath during all the time I spoke. The words 'William' and 'Simon' always proved hard for me to say. The love I felt for them was overwhelming but when I thanked everyone on their behalf I knew I'd said enough and any more would make me cry. I put my head down and walked quietly back to my seat. The audience rose to their feet and gave me a standing ovation. It was too much. Pete walked up and put his arms round me.

'Simon would have been so proud. He'd have looked down and said, "My wife spoke at the AHAC and got a standing ovation!"' He was also close to tears. 'Now let's go to the bar – Simon would have said that too!'

On the last day of the trip Pete and I were invited for lunch with Joe Benoit. We met at Joe's favourite seafood restaurant overlooking Boston Harbour. The sun was shining and the food was excellent.

'Can I tell you a story?' Joe asked. 'It's about my wife, Marilyn, and what happened to her on 11 September. It's why we both feel that you're a very special friend of ours, Elizabeth.'

Marilyn was scheduled to fly out to Los Angeles on Wednesday, 12 September to see her mother Catherine who had been taken seriously ill. When she arrived at the office on the morning of 10 September it suddenly occurred to her that she hadn't yet made arrangements for a car at the airport. While placing the call to the car rental company, she fished the airline ticket out of her briefcase and discovered that the travel agent had made a mistake: the ticket she held was for American Airlines Flight 11, departing Boston at 7.50 a.m. on Tuesday, 11 September. Marilyn had a powerful instinct to change it and called the travel agent immediately to rectify the mistake.

'When American Flight 11 flew into the World Trade Center the next day,' said Joe, 'we both knew immediately that Marilyn should have been on it. For weeks afterwards she relived the moments of September 10th, feeling that a guardian angel was with her, urging her on to get that ticket exchanged. She still has dreams in which she walks down the aisle of that plane, touching the passengers.'

Silence fell across the table.

'Marilyn and I now live each day as a gift and a blessing,' he finished.

I was beginning to understand the feeling of connection I'd had when I first met Joe.

He reached over and put his hand on my arm. 'We were just friends who hadn't met yet,' he concluded.

I don't think I'd considered that anything would really come of it, but Cherie Blair was true to her word. After I got back from Boston, she invited us to Downing Street for tea.

I decided I wanted to be fairly smart, so I wore a black suit, a silver top that had been part of my 'going away' outfit when we got married, and the diamond necklace Simon had given me. It was simple, but included Simon, and I was pleased with how I looked.

Jan, William and I drove to Number 10 in Jan's little white Vauxhall Corsa. As we approached Downing Street Jan asked, 'Where do I go now?'

'I think you just turn right across Whitehall,' I said, giggling.

I was sitting in a steamed-up car on a soaking wet day with a six-month-old baby about to go and meet the Prime Minister's wife. Not really an everyday event for most new mums!

We were welcomed into the building and shown into a waiting room. I had imagined we'd be taken to one of the state rooms, which worried me as I wasn't sure how baby-friendly they'd be. However, as Jan and I were led through a maze of corridors we found ourselves on a large landing full of toys.

William's eyes lit up before we were taken into a sun-filled lounge and told to make ourselves comfortable.

'Jan,' I whispered, 'we're in the private home. This is Eleven Downing Street, not Number Ten!'

We both looked around at all the family photographs and personal items that define a home.

'I can't believe it,' I told Jan, 'their curtains are made from the same material as mine!' We laughed out loud and quickly took some photographs of William and me standing in front of the curtains for my 'parallel universe' photo album back at home.

Cherie soon joined us. 'It's so lovely to meet you,' she said. 'And you must be William Turner!'

Cherie disarmed me with her warmth and informality. I'd read so much in the papers about her and the way she came across but found myself instead drinking tea at the kitchen table with another mum in a pair of slippers with curlers in her hair.

'Sorry about the curlers but I've got a charity function tonight and I wanted to have as much time with you as I could.'

I laughed and suddenly felt completely overdressed for the occasion. Cherie asked all about Simon and what had happened to him; we talked about William's birth and she told me about her children and what they were doing with their lives. Ewan and Catherine both came in to meet William, and Catherine held him while we talked together. I relaxed and enjoyed it, and left feeling that I'd spent the afternoon with friends, which was so much more than I'd anticipated.

Chapter Twelve

To me it didn't feel as though 11 September had ever gone away during that first year. I lived with it every single day – the absence of Simon, the presence of our child, and always some legal, financial or emotional fallout from the event to deal with. So when the anniversary came along I was shocked by the amount of attention that came from the press. Once again the phone started ringing, journalists started knocking on the door and the papers began to build up the picture one year on from the event.

The onslaught really began in August and I received an email from a friend asking if I'd seen the *Mail on Sunday* that day. He felt I should know what had been printed so that I was prepared. Astonishingly, they had taken the pictures of the people who'd jumped from the building on 11 September ('jumpers' as they were termed) and enlarged them so that the individuals could be identified.

I felt sick. I hated the papers for forcing me to confront such an issue before the anniversary. Why would the press do something like this? I'd always wondered if Simon had been one of those people. I couldn't bear the idea that one of the pictures might be of him.

I went downstairs and told Jan about what had happened.

'It's always been your greatest fear about Simon's death,' she reminded me.

'If you don't face it completely, it'll keep coming back until you do. What difference will it make if you know that that's what Simon did?'

'No difference, but it still devastates me that he may have had to make that decision,' I replied. 'Worst of all is the fear that I might see an image of it.'

'It's like when you received the death certificates. It would just confirm in a different way something you already know. You'd be completing a bit more of the jigsaw of information surrounding Simon's death. Do you want more information or not?'

Jan was always able to guide me back to the bigger picture and remind me that I had choices. Throughout the last year this had continually helped me to reconnect with my power when I thought it had been taken away from me. I felt that the newspapers were taking my control away with this potential information about Simon's death, but now I remembered that I knew Simon was dead and that I could choose how much more I needed to complete the picture. This perspective had often helped me as I asked myself, for example, whether I wanted to do any interviews, or go to a memorial service. I was able to accept the choices I made and keep my power. I had already decided that it didn't matter how he died. I respected any choice he'd made on the day. I also believed it was a deeply private thing, and something that shouldn't be witnessed and pored over by anyone. But if it was there and other people were going to see it, then I had to as well.

I walked slowly down the street towards the newsagents,

hating the press as I went. I bought the paper and immediately turned to the pages and read them as I walked back home. Simon's picture wasn't there.

I chose Jill and Jan to come with me to New York for the first anniversary. My brothers and sisters all had responsibilities and Jane's children were back at school. Celine told me flatly that she didn't want to go. I wanted Jan there to help me with the practicalities of looking after William. Jill and Jan knew more than anyone how much I had learnt in the last year and I knew they would understand my response to the anniversary.

That first night in New York I wasn't completely sure about how I felt. On the one hand I hated the fact that Simon, William and I had to be part of this event as it meant that something awful had happened to us, and yet on the other it felt profoundly important and moving to be part of it, particularly after everything I had learnt.

My family were going to be attending a memorial service at St Paul's Cathedral in London but I instinctively knew that I needed to be in New York. I also knew that I wouldn't repeat this on any future anniversary so it needed to be absolutely right. I wanted to be able to tell William when he was older that he had been there at the anniversary within Ground Zero to remember his dad. These parts of the equation were hugely important to me. There could be no 'what ifs'.

What I wore on these important dates had become a big part of the ritual. On the morning of the anniversary I got dressed in a black stripy top I'd worn on my first date with Simon to see *Men in Black* in Islington. I put on the earrings Simon gave me for our wedding, along with my wedding band

and engagement ring. Then I added a medal that the HAC had awarded to Simon for long service. He was very proud of it, and it felt important to wear it to say how proud I was of him too and to mark his courage on that day.

Jan, Jill, William and I went on the bus down to Ground Zero. The day replicated itself for the anniversary. The sky was a brilliant blue and there wasn't a cloud to be seen. The weather was warm and still and it was a beautiful end to summer – just like the year before. The traffic was actually quite bad that morning but it gave us time to look at all the memorials that had been put up in the shop windows. There were displays of white flowers and the Stars and Stripes, and the words 'We remember' were emblazoned everywhere. It was a day of remembrance for the whole city and not just for the relatives of the people who had died.

It had been reported that they were expecting about 5000 people at Ground Zero but in fact over 20,000 came to pay their respects. It was only immediate family and friends who were given access to Ground Zero so all the people I was standing with had lost someone close to them or their family. It was unbelievable to see the numbers of people. It gave me a poignant perspective on the event I was linked with.

We had to walk slowly in the enormous queue as even though we all wore badges to show we were registered it still took a long time to process so many people through the gates and into the footprint of the World Trade Center. I was beginning to panic. I needed to be at Ground Zero at 8.46 a.m. This was the moment the first plane hit the building and therefore the first time the event had an impact on Simon. I had to be in his footsteps as best as I could and needed to be there to hear the bell at the right time. These expectations I'd put on myself weren't helpful, but I knew they were important parts of my journey forward.

Of course, I had underestimated the American machine, which had impressed me so much in the immediate aftermath. The queue speeded up and we were tagged through the gate and pointed in the direction of the family viewing area and the Red Cross who were handing out refreshments of water, cookies and fruit. Jan, Jill, William and I met up with the three Family Liaison Officers who were supporting the British families and they walked around with us until we found a good place to stand and watch the ceremony. William was enthralled by their pens and shiny badges, which allowed me space to take in the experience.

As I looked around I could see people carrying photographs, flowers, American flags and personal quotes and messages. People had printed their loved ones' pictures on to their shirts and jackets and others carried huge placards with messages to the people they'd lost. I had nothing with me other than my son, Simon's medal and my friends. My heart held all my messages for Simon and I knew that I'd send them silently to him throughout the day.

The ceremony was very simple. A bell sounded to mark the moment each plane hit and each tower fell. There was a minute's silence and then the Gettysburg Address was read out. It was very subtle and very respectful. There were no religious connotations and no judgements given about the day and the people involved. It was purely to remember the people who were lost. The mothers, fathers, wives, husbands, brothers, sisters, sons and daughters . . . I thought of Simon and the friends who'd been with him. I had met a number of them and now they were gone, connected forever by the manner and time of their death.

It had been warm and still up to that point, so incredibly still in fact, that everyone could clearly hear the bell resonate around Ground Zero and in the minute's silence I heard a cough from the other side of the footprint of the World Trade Center. But as they began to read out the names of everyone that died, a wind suddenly picked up out of nowhere. It blew upward into a huge dust cloud and whirled around within the footprint like a mini tornado. Everyone stood and watched it. I had a powerful feeling that the 2974 people who had died were making their presence felt.

Next the wind caught the huge American flag that was held in place on the side of the building towering behind us. The flag was enormous and the wind pulled at it so much that one of the ropes holding it came away. Finally, as a board whipped high above our heads, dancing in the wind, the US flag was ripped in half. It said so much.

There were so many people who died that day that it felt as though the wind were made up of all of their energy. I suppose a normal observer would explain it as a twist of fate but I had witnessed too many unbelievable coincidences.

I started to walk down into the footprint of Ground Zero so that I could hear Simon's name being read out while I was down there. I'd decided to leave a cream rose from me and a pink one from William, and wrote a note to Simon.

It was 10.26 a.m. and the bell rang for the fourth and last time. We all observed the minute's silence when the second tower fell, which was when I believe Simon actually died.

I walked down the ramp with William in my arms. I held him tight to protect him from the dust, but actually it was me that needed the closeness more than him. I laid the flowers on the memorial that was set up in the centre of the foundations and then once again the wind blew strongly, covering us all in a thin film of dust. We were just like all the people a year ago, white and ghostly after the buildings collapsed.

I thought I might feel a surge of emotion or that I might cry or be overcome but in fact I felt calm. I looked around. People were sitting crying on the ground, hugging each other; a family were awkwardly carrying the most enormous flower arrangement to place at the memorial; and there were others like me, standing and watching in disbelief. I listened to the names as they were read out. I was familiar with the two people who came before Simon in alphabetical order and in some strange way I almost thought of them as Simon's friends now. I heard their names: '. . . Lance Richard Tumulty, Ching Ping Tung . . .'

And then a man's voice said loud and clear, '. . . Simon James Turner . . .'

Time seemed to stand still. I felt everything around me stop and as I looked up at the huge American flag on the building opposite, the sun shone brightly. For a brief moment, it was just me and Simon, locked together in our love and our sadness. I cried and with the tears the world started moving again.

I left my message to Simon on the wall of Ground Zero as so many other people were doing, so that when they filled up the foundations it would always be there. Little things like this mattered. I felt that in some way Simon was being remembered within the depths of the place where he'd died. I also picked up an empty water bottle and, copying others, filled it with dirt. This was an interesting thing to do because I wasn't actually sure that I wanted dirt from this place. But in the spirit of getting it absolutely right I scraped up the mud and pushed it into the tiny bottle. My hands were filthy and I felt very self-conscious, but I reasoned that if I didn't take it and then wanted some later it would be upsetting. This way, if I found I didn't want to keep it I could throw it away. There was method in my madness.

It had taken two and a half hours simply to read out all the names, and now it was time to leave. I took one last look around and then silently said goodbye.

Chapter Thirteen

The first year after Simon's death had felt like an adrenalin-fuelled rollercoaster ride. I wasn't well after I got back from New York. I felt drained of energy, exhausted and pale, and everything hurt and ached. If nothing else I knew that, physically, the last year had taken its toll.

Jan had left and was now working with another family but we remained very close. After seeing Dad at Simon's memorial service I spent a lot of time with my parents. It gave William the opportunity to get to know his grandparents, and it gave me the chance to finish building bridges. Mum and I talked a lot. I knew that I had to find peace with her. Simon's death had made me realize that life was too short not to enjoy a relationship that was such an important part of my life.

Soon after my first trip to New York I went in to Channel 4 to meet Peter, my boss there. My maternity leave didn't end until August, and technically I wouldn't have to share any decisions I'd made until then, but Channel 4 had been exceptionally supportive and kind and I wanted to ensure they were aware of everything a long time before it actually happened. I felt certain that they would have accommodated any flexibility in my working hours to help with William and my situation, but I knew this wouldn't be fair, either for them or me.

I thanked them for everything and explained why I had to leave. Peter was very understanding and made my decision much easier.

There was still a lot to sort out, but I knew I also needed to rest and allow the shock to pass through my body. I had read many articles about the mind, body, spirit connection and I was beginning to respect the impact grief could have. I understood that shock and trauma could leave a scar on the body and that I needed to help myself absorb the experience – and then forgive it. I knew that this would take time, patience and study. It was time to create some peace and quiet for myself.

I was trying to enjoy a few extra moments in bed one Saturday morning when the phone rang.

'Elizabeth, I'm really sorry but Mum passed away this morning,' Dad told me calmly.

I sat in silence. I didn't know what to say. We all knew that Mum was very ill but it was one of those illnesses where she could have died that day, or it might not have happened for another ten years. I thought I'd had my quota of mountains to climb over the last year, but clearly that wasn't to be the case. Within eighteen months my husband had died, my son had been born and now Mum had died. The question was, what had I really learnt in that time that would support me during this experience?

I put the phone down. I was lost for words, so I called Jan.

'Jan, my mum died this morning.' As I said the words, the tears began to fall. 'William and I are driving up to Dad's this morning. I don't know what'll happen after that but at least I'll be there and I can help Dad with any arrangements.' I resorted to thinking about all the things that needed doing. Jan caught me then.

'Elizabeth, you've always told me you'd said everything you wanted to say to your mum as you knew she was ill. This is your opportunity to use everything you've learnt since Simon died. As you drive up to Leeds, take the time to think about all the wonderful things you remember about your mum before she got ill and to say thank you for everything she's done for you in your life.'

I knew it was the perfect opportunity but at that point all I could think about was that Dad had told me he would keep Mum at the house so that I could say goodbye to her properly. This was quite a shock. Dad was Protestant by faith and I understood this custom to be Roman Catholic and had never experienced it. I had never seen a dead body before either, and even though it was my mum I wasn't sure I wanted to be put in this situation.

William and I were the last to arrive at Dad's house. Deborah, Catherine and Mark had already been to see Mum.

I was terrified of going upstairs. I had no idea what to expect or how I'd react. However, I did know that 'what ifs' were bad to have left so I knew I'd regret it if I didn't go to see her.

I walked up the stairs and took a deep breath. If there was ever a time to use my Reiki techniques, this was it. I walked slowly, and breathed the Reiki energy into my stomach where the nerves were developing and quietly asked to have the experience I needed to help me absorb my mum's death. I visualized a beautiful gold light surrounding me to represent the love I wanted to take in for my mum and I found myself at the bedroom door.

I stood outside and breathed deep into the calm water I visualized in my stomach. It was still and deep and I remembered my quote again:

Peace. It does not mean to be in a place where there is no noise, trouble or hard work. It means to be in the midst of those things and still be calm in your heart.

I put my hand on the door handle and walked into the bedroom.

Mum was lying on her side of the bed with her eyes closed and her arms by her side. It was quiet in the bedroom, the curtains moving gently in the breeze from the open window. Mum didn't like sleeping with the windows shut. It felt claustrophobic. I could hear the neighbours cutting their lawn and, in the distance, children's laughter as they played in the sunshine. The sky was a beautiful deep blue. I looked back at the bed. She looked like my mum but there was something very important missing: the vitality and vivaciousness of the woman I'd loved. The body was still and white and it looked like a model.

As I stood and stared, I felt happy. I could see very clearly that Mum had left her body behind. It was there lying in front of me but her spirit had gone. I was standing in the bedroom with an empty shell and it made me happy. I immediately knew that Mum had physically gone but her spirit was still out there.

I took Mum's hand, sat on the side of the bed and talked to her.

I went back downstairs with the rest of the family and not long after that the undertakers arrived. We all waited nervously in the lounge as they took Mum out of the house. Dad,

Deborah, Mark, Catherine and I followed them out and watched as they carried her down the drive to the waiting car. I had William in my arms and as they walked away he began to wave.

'Bye, bye,' he said. I cried.

Chapter Fourteen

William and I had had a wonderful summer holiday enjoying the end of his first school year. We were over the fifth anniversary. I had nearly completed all my Reiki and life-coaching qualifications and had tentatively stepped back into the world of work while managing William's first experience of education. It had been stressful getting to know the school and parents, and how it all worked, and doing lots of play dates. As a single parent I had to juggle everything. I was exhausted by the end of it and William was too. But he'd loved it and had achieved so many things at such a young age. He could read and write, he could ice-skate, he'd made lots of friends and he'd thrown himself into the whole year. Life was looking good and it was exciting.

But there was one cloud in the blue sky that was bothering me. I had spoken to Catherine about it at the beginning of the summer when we went to Cornwall for our holiday.

I had got to a certain point with the explanation of Simon's death to William, but I was worried that someone would tell him things before I had the chance. Catherine convinced me that this wouldn't happen and that people were more sensitive than that. However, I knew a couple of friends who had told their children about 11 September and more than anything I wanted to tell William when he was ready and not when my hand was forced. I respected and valued Catherine's view, but I still worried that it might come out accidentally.

I had decided that I would answer William's questions about his father's death as and when he asked them. It would be easy for me to give him all the information I had but I knew that he needed to ask the questions when they came up in his understanding. There were a number of different stages to this questioning.

When William was about two years old he realized that his friends had daddies but he didn't.

'Where is my daddy?' he asked.

'Your daddy is dead,' I replied.

William would ask one question and I gave him one answer then waited to see whether he needed to ask another. Most of the time at the beginning one answer was enough and kept him happy for a few months.

Then William started nursery. I sat down with the nursery staff and explained how Simon had died so that they'd understand if William said anything or got upset. They were very understanding and considerate. They asked if William would like to make a Grandfather's Day card on Father's Day and this worked really well, with William proudly coming out carrying his card and announcing to the world that he had a granddad card because his daddy had died. I always encouraged open communication about Simon with William but watched as other people flinched or squirmed in discomfort when they listened to him talking about his dad. It was definitely their discomfort and not William's. He liked to talk about his daddy and I felt that it was healthy.

One day I was taken to one side by the nursery nurse when I arrived to pick William up for lunch.

'Mrs Turner, could I have a word?' I was going to get very used to that phrase before people told me about something William had said about his dad.

'Today, we were talking about fire engines and William told us that his dad was a fireman. We didn't realize he was but he did say that he died on a building site.' I had to laugh when they told me. I could see that a fireman was a much better career option for his dad in William's eyes!

I realized that some of my explanations had gone a bit haywire. I needed to go back to the drawing board. It was challenging and came with a huge responsibility. I had to make sure that my son's explanation of his father's death was clear, honest and healthy. I vowed that whatever I was doing or whenever I was doing it, if William asked a question I had to stop and answer it there and then.

There were times during the 'Spanish Inquisitions' that William subjected me to when I laughed, times when I was emotionally neutral and times when I could have sobbed for the rest of my life. I looked into his earnest brown eyes, knowing that there was nothing I could do to help him other than to be gentle, loving and there for him. He had to learn these lessons on his own. I had to let him feel his own emotions and work it all out so that he could decide what the experience meant to him.

Interestingly, the next phase of questioning began when William was about four. We were driving down the North Circular in London after going to the cinema together to watch the Disney cartoon film *Ice Age 2*.

'Can I ask you a question, Mummy?' William asked as we drove along the busy road.

'Of course,' I replied, expecting something about woolly mammoths or melting ice caps.

'Who killed my daddy?' he asked calmly.

I felt the car swerve and my stomach lurched. We hadn't had any questions for a good nine months and it was shocking to be asked something as direct as this. I was taken by surprise at the new line in the questioning. I had no idea where he'd got the idea that his dad had been killed by someone. We had only approached the fact that Simon had died when the buildings he was working in had fallen down.

I took a deep breath. I felt a powerful responsibility to get this answer right, but I wasn't even sure what it looked like in this context. How could I present this to William and show him that life is positive if I was about to give him an example of how cruel the world can be? I didn't want to spread more hatred or create the potential for revenge but I also wanted to be honest.

'Some people from another country killed your daddy,' I replied. Then I waited.

Silence. The noise of a little four-year-old processing the details of his dad's death at the hands of other people. What would he ask next, I wondered?

'If they hadn't killed my daddy, would my daddy still be alive?' he asked.

'Yes, he would, William,' I replied clearly again.

I kept my eyes on the road and didn't look at him. I had remembered from when I was a little girl that it's always easier to ask the hardest questions or admit to doing something when you're not looking directly at someone. Whenever any of my siblings or I were troubled Mum would create an opportunity for us to walk up on the hills with Dad and the dog. When you walk side by side you're not looking at each other and it's easier to talk from your heart.

I stole a quick look into the back seat to see my little boy staring out of the car window. I left him with that thought.

We returned home and I was rattled. I made a good cup of Yorkshire tea and sat down. William raced through the kitchen and outside to play in the garden.

'Mummy, can you take the sand-pit cover off for me?' he shouted.

I removed the lid for William and set about picking weeds from the borders of my garden and tidying away some of the dead branches from the lawn after the winter storms. I often enjoyed the air outside, the wind and the opportunity to feel the space when my thoughts were crowded in my head. It helped me to let some of them go. The wind could take them and the rain could wash them away, and the fresh air always helped to make some sense of the jumble of thoughts or the pressures of responsibility.

'Mummy!' William shouted.

'Yes?' I replied, lost in what had happened earlier.

'So, will someone kill me when I get older too? Just like Daddy?'

I realized that this was a complex thought process and that thankfully the approach I was taking with William at the moment was wholly appropriate. I hadn't expected this question because I couldn't predict the way his mind worked. If I'd thought about it, I'd have expected him to want to know more about the men who killed his daddy, but in fact the connections he'd made were about his own mortality. It was a really good example of how important it was not to put my own emotional slant on William's interpretation. I should never try to tell him what he was thinking. It was my responsibility to give him the freedom to think and feel his way to what he needed to do.

'It's unusual for someone to die young at all, sweetheart,' I replied, trying to stall him and give myself time to create an answer. 'Most people live until they're old and they die from old age or because they're ill. It's very unusual for anyone to be killed by someone else at any age,' I explained carefully.

Silence. And I waited.

'Will you be killed?' William asked.

'It would be very unusual for that to happen to me, William,' I told him. I needed to tell him the truth but not to promise something I couldn't keep.

'Was Daddy surprised to be killed?' William wondered.

'Yes, I think we can safely say that it wasn't on his agenda! We were all surprised, William, because it's so unusual,' I replied.

Silence again. This time I waited and waited. But William had had enough for the moment. Eventually he would find all the pieces for his jigsaw puzzle and then he would work out how it all fitted together. When it was complete it would be the picture of his father's death. I would help him as best I could but the greatest education for me was that this was William's puzzle and he had to collect the pieces and work it out for himself. If I tried to do it for him then I'd be denying him the opportunity to work out who he was and how he felt about the situation. It was the greatest gift I could give him as a mother – as long as I was able to stick to my plan.

I decided it was time to visit the local Muswell Hill children's bookshop to ask for their recommendations for stories that helped children understand grief. I realized that William's questions weren't the only avenue for him to get answers and that we should explore as many as possible. I bought some books about people dying and we started our own little library that allowed William to read with me whenever he liked.

There was a favourite book of mine that William loved too.

'This book reminds me of my daddy,' he would always say as he pulled it off the bookshelf. 'I love the water bugs and dragonfly story.'

The story described a group of water bugs at the bottom of a river who couldn't understand why every now and then one of their group disappeared up the water-lily stem and never came back. They all agreed to make a pact for the next one who went up the stem to return and explain what was happening. The next water bug found himself climbing up the stem and when he woke up he was lying on the lily pad and had turned into a dragonfly. He flew around in the air and wondered at the beauty of his situation. He suddenly caught a glimpse of his friends the water bugs down below and remembered his promise. He stopped in his tracks as he realized that he couldn't go back because he would drown if he went in the water. And the water bugs wouldn't recognize him anyway, now that he was in a different form. So he decided to wait until the next water bugs came up the stem and then he would be able to explain everything. This story helped William to understand that his dad was around watching him but was in a different form and on a different energy level.

I also realized that it would be a good idea to introduce William to other people who had lost their parents. I was able to tell him that Jan's sons didn't have a daddy, that my mum had died and that even Granddad, Prince William and Prince Harry had lost their mums when they were young. It was essential to show William that he wasn't different from everybody else, and that other people were in the same situation as him.

William told me regularly how much he missed his daddy and I always replied in the same way.

'I think your daddy must miss you too. I also miss him but I know that he loved me and you very much and he knows how many great people we have around us in our family and among our friends to help us and to help you when you need him. Your godparents are your daddy's best friends, so they can tell you stories about him and you can learn as much as possible about him. And there are lots of his friends around who you'll get to know when you're older and who will support you. They loved your daddy very much and they want to help you as much as they can too.'

I was never sure how much of this William took in but I was convinced that if I said it often enough he'd realize one day that there were a lot of people around him to talk to if he didn't want to talk to me.

As time moved on I began to realize that William might end up as an only child. I was in my mid-thirties and the truth was that unless I met someone fast the possibilities of having another child were getting smaller. I was the youngest of four children, so I'd always thought that having no siblings might be a sad thing for William. But I'd also learnt that it was important to look at the things I did have, rather than mourn the things I didn't. I had William and he had his cousin Pippy, Ron and Catherine's daughter. William and Pippy were only five weeks apart and many people thought they were twins. It was a wonderful relationship that I knew was going to be important to William as he grew older.

As an only child, William had the opportunity to spend a lot of time with me and to have a lot of my attention. This was a plus for him but it also meant that the relationship was quite intense and I felt it would be healthy to dilute that if I could.

I already had two cats I'd inherited from Simon, called Azzy and Maya. William and I loved them dearly but they were moving into their senior years and spent most of their time sleeping. They had taught William the valuable lesson of the difference between animals and toys. When you grab a toy and drag it out from under the bed, it doesn't generally flick its claws out and give you a good swipe. There were many tears but I consistently and calmly told William that Azzy and Maya were living creatures and that if he scared them or hurt them they would hurt him back. It wasn't long before I regularly came across him lying with one of them in the upstairs corridor stroking them and whispering secrets into their soft fur.

I began to think that it might be an idea to bring a puppy into our lives. I had always been brought up with dogs. William's granddad had a beautiful Golden Retriever called George, my sister had a Springer Spaniel and a black Labrador called Dan and Jake and my neighbour had a stunning Novia Scotia Duck Tolling Retriever called Charlie. William was spending a lot of time with dogs and enjoyed the running around and playing involved with them. He knew not to stroke a strange dog without asking the owner first, and he knew not to go near a dog when they were eating or sleeping. He was learning the rules of pet ownership without realizing it.

After a lot of research I decided the best dog for us would be a Blue Roan Cocker Spaniel. My sister and I phoned the Kennel Club and got lots of contact numbers, only to be faced with litter after litter being reserved because next to the yellow Labrador I had chosen the most popular breed in the UK. I felt a bit disillusioned but resolved to be patient and trust that the right dog would come to us when it was good and ready. I realized that I could cope with the waiting but William probably couldn't, so I kept Project Puppy a secret.

After several months and many false starts, I heard about a lady in Putney whose bitch was expecting a litter. I gave her a ring. Victoria Hunt was fairly unimpressed by the idea of handing over one of her puppies to a single parent with a four-year-old boy. I explained the reasoning behind my getting a dog and why I thought it would be special and important in William's life. She understood but still asked me to bring William down to meet the puppies.

My neighbour, Helen, helped me out and pretended to be going to look at a puppy for herself, asking whether William and I would like to go with her. William was very excited.

The visit went really well, with William pulling out all the stops and showing how careful and respectful he was of animals. Helen and I breathed a sigh of relief. I was very proud of him and as soon as we got home I phoned Victoria.

'I can't think of a better family for one of my puppies to go to!' she said. 'I think that the best puppy for you would be Spot.'

I couldn't believe what she'd said.

'What did you just call the puppy?' I asked.

'Spot. Don't worry, though. We just use names that help us distinguish the puppy and this one has a white spot on his head. You can call him whatever you want. In fact if you tell us the name we'll start using it for him straight away.'

I couldn't speak.

'Elizabeth, are you still there?' Victoria asked.

I felt quite tearful as I explained about Simon and his joke when I was pregnant and how William had been Spot until he was born. And I kept thinking, 'I waited and I was patient and the right dog has arrived.'

It was Victoria's turn to be speechless.

'Spot is definitely going to the right home,' she said eventually.

Archie (as we named him) settled in quickly and it wasn't long before he was part of the regular comings and goings of the Turner household. William was very excited at first but the competition, as he saw it, started to bother him and he began to see Archie not as a friend but as someone he had to share his mum with.

Whenever I left William on his own in a room, he went in search of the puppy and pulled his tail or his ears – things that hurt him. There had been many people in our lives since Simon died but Archie was the only one that had moved in permanently and William changed his mind about sharing his mum. It was a difficult period and it got to the point when I thought I might have to give Archie back.

Helen came round the following day and said that her daughter had made an interesting observation.

'If Elizabeth sends Archie away then William has got what he wants,' she'd said.

That made me think. If in the future somebody came into my life then William would have this problem all over again. I realized I had to deal with it there and then.

William came home from nursery and I waited until he had a go at Archie. Then I explained that there was enough love to go round and that hurting Archie wasn't acceptable. I got down to William's eye level and said, 'William, I love you and I love Archie. However, because I love you I'm not going to let you carry on hurting Archie. From now on, he's my dog and not ours.' I told him that until he could learn to share the love between the three of us he would be separated from me and Archie.

It was very tough, but I knew it was right to show William how adult relationships worked. He needed to understand that love could be shared and the more you give out the more you get back, rather than the more you give out the less there is. We had a bumpy week and then William began to understand what it all meant. The hurting stopped, the separations stopped and we began to spend time together as a family. William and Archie are now best friends. Archie runs to meet William from school, they hug together, William walks him, trains him, gives him treats and includes him in his games and, best of all, he tells his friends how to look after animals.

It was story time and William and I were lying on his bed reading a children's story called 'The Mountains of Tibet' which interprets the Buddhist teachings on reincarnation. William read about how an old man died and then got to choose which universe, star, planet, country and family he would be born back into. He had to decide whether to be an animal or a child and whether to be a boy or a girl. It was a lovely simple story and William often asked to read it.

'Mummy, do you think that my daddy has come back as something?' he asked.

'No, I think he's waiting in heaven until you go there so that he can keep an eye on you,' I replied without thinking.

'I think Daddy has come back as something,' he said, staring at me intently.

'Oh. OK. What do you think he's come back as?'

'Archie.'

I laughed. I could see Simon looking quite indignant at the thought of coming back as a small black and white cocker spaniel. Not quite his style!

'I don't think he's Archie. I think he's in heaven so that he can look after you and keep you safe.'

William thought for a while. 'That's what Archie does, so I do think Daddy has come back as Archie to watch over me here,' he concluded.

I wasn't sure what to say to that but remembered that it wasn't my right to judge what William was thinking, and to be quite honest who was I to say that Simon hadn't come back as Archie? I had learnt in the last few years to let people have their own experience and not to judge them for it.

I gave William a huge hug.

'Well, when you put it like that, then maybe you're right.'

I looked at Archie and he looked back at me. He does have exactly the same colour eyes as Simon!

*   *   *

It was the last week before William returned to school for his second year. We were having a quiet week at home enjoying the rest before the new term started, but had arranged to meet William's friend, George, for a day running around on Hampstead Heath. Despite the summer of rain and flooding the last few days of the holiday were suddenly warm and sunny so we thought a picnic and a big adventure in the woods would be great fun for the boys. George and his sister Lilli, his mum Jenny, William and I all set off for a lovely day out. The boys ran around pretending to catch dragons and dinosaurs and they picked up sticks and used them to battle against the various imaginary animals that surrounded them. They ran in and out of the woods, protected Lilli from all the scary monsters and had one of those idyllic childhood play times that involves the outdoors, nature, imagination and props that you can only find in a wood. It was proving to be a magical summer's day.

Jenny and I walked among the trees, keeping an eye on our energetic sons, making sure they included Lilli in their games and didn't run too far away. We eventually stopped for lunch on a green patch of grass within the wood where there was a bench and, best of all, a fallen tree which we knew would keep the boys entertained for hours when they'd had enough to eat.

We laid out the food and the children descended on it like a plague of locusts, before disappearing off to explore the tree. Jenny and I talked and as I looked around I felt the enjoyment of the moment and absorbed the end of the summer months. It felt different this year. I had finished my coaching course and established lots of new clients, and thought I might concentrate on writing a book of my journey as well as growing my business. William was really settled and I felt we were in a good place to move forward.

I could hear William and George shouting in the distance as they played spacemen or pirates on the tree. I listened to their joyful shouts. Then I listened closer and suddenly felt that cold fear that only a mother knows as I realized that the sound I could hear was not shouting but screaming. Adrenalin surged through my limbs as I ran as fast as I could.

I hurtled towards the fallen tree and as I did George ran towards me with a terrified look on his face. I felt sick.

'William is hurt!' shouted George.

'Please don't let anything have happened to William!' I whispered to myself as I ran.

I had no idea what to expect. I could see William standing inside the roots of the fallen tree but I had no idea what was happening to him. He was shaking with fear and had his hands and arms wrapped around his body as though he were trying to protect himself from something.

'William!' I screamed and he turned to me with a petrified look on his face.

'I can't get out and the wasps are stinging me,' he cried.

I was terrified.

By this point, Jenny had run over to me and she grabbed my arm. She looked me straight in the face and said, with the tone that only a great friend can, 'Elizabeth, we're not going to panic about this, are we?'

I looked at her and realized that we were the adults and that William would look to me to know how to respond to this situation. How I behaved when he came to me would dictate how this would all go. I had to snap out of terrified mummy mode and be very calm and in control. I immediately swallowed my fear back down into my stomach. I quickly worked out a way through the roots and gently talked William through the branches towards me. I cast my eyes over him to see what was going on and realized that he was covered in wasps. It was late summer and they were drowsy and hooked on to his clothes. As I flicked them to knock them away they weren't coming off. They were trapped and angry and they were stinging William for all they were worth.

I managed to get hold of William's arm and walked him towards me. 'William, look at me. I am here now and I am going to sort this out but I need you to do everything I ask you to. I need to strip all of your clothes off as the wasps are hooked on the material. I am going to take them off and then we're going to run over to that bench and leave your clothes here.'

He nodded his head and looked at me with his tear-streaked face. He gave me all of his trust and let me do what I needed to do. He was relying on me to protect him and keep him safe.

I stripped off his jacket, T-shirt, trousers and socks and picked him up in my arms and ran as fast as I could to the bench. He was sobbing so hard I could feel every part of his body shaking. He had gone into shock and the colour was draining from his face. I held him in my arms and told him over and over again, 'The wasps aren't on you any more. You're safe now.'

Jenny had taken William's clothes and beaten them until every single wasp had either dropped off or been brutally squashed. We had to show him each item before he would trust me to put them back on.

All I could think of was what his reaction would be to the

wasps' stings. Somehow Jenny and I carried a wasp-stung boy, two traumatized friends, a subdued dog and a bag of picnic things across the heath and back to the car.

That evening, William's face swelled up and after an examination with my neighbour Helen, who routinely came over in her pyjamas to help me diagnose any of William's illnesses, we agreed to visit A & E. The doctor there said that his body was responding the way it should and although it looked awful he was just fighting the poison from the stings and should be fine with antihistamines to take away the scratching. Back at the house I searched through my cupboards for the homeopathic remedy aconite to treat him for shock. I was about to put the bottle back in the cupboard when Archie caught my eye, lying in his basket. He was shocked too so I gave him a drop of aconite as well! It had been an exhausting experience and William and I curled up on the sofa together. I gave him a tight hug and realized he was crying.

'You're safe now, sweetheart,' I told him quietly.

'I really miss my daddy,' William sobbed.

'I know you do and I bet your daddy misses you,' I told him, trying to comfort him in what was clearly a no-win situation.

'I wish he was here after the wasp attack,' he cried.

'Of all days, I think your daddy would want to be here to help you after something like this,' I explained.

I didn't see the next question coming at all.

'How did those men knock those buildings down? Did they use hammers?'

'No,' I replied, desperately trying to move my brain from wasp attacks to terrorist attacks and find some stable ground in this turbulent afternoon.

'Did they use pickaxes or balls on chains?' he continued, warming to his theme.

'No, they didn't use those either.'

'So what did they use, then?' William asked, looking me directly in the eye.

I knew this was it. This was the moment I had been thinking about since William was born. This was the moment that would give William all the key pieces to the jigsaw. This was the moment that in my mind was the most important one in William's understanding of his future.

'They used planes, William,' I told him. If he wanted to talk about this now, then we would. There would be no fobbing him off or telling him not to think about it or to rest after his shock. The wasp attack had triggered something in this five-year-old boy's mind about his father's death and today was the day he wanted to know it all. Today was the day I had to tell him about it.

'Was it an accident?'

'No.'

'Did they do it on purpose?'

'Yes, they did.'

'Did the buildings catch fire?'

'Yes, they did.'

'Can I see them? Are they still on fire?'

I didn't expect William to ask that question.

'The buildings aren't on fire now, William, as this all happened before you were born. They were on fire but then the buildings collapsed. You can see where the buildings used to stand and I will take you to see them one day.'

'Why can't I see them now?'

'Do you want to see them now?'

'It's just a long time until I'm older when I can see them.'

I decided not to answer that question then but thought that if William asked to see Ground Zero again in the future I'd have to start thinking about a trip to New York to take him.

'Did you watch the buildings on television?' William continued.

'Yes, I did.' I was puzzled by this question.

'I knew that it must have been on television because how else would you have known that Daddy was in it?' he confirmed to himself.

William was a child of the twenty-first century and I realized that in his mind, any communication must be done via the television or some medium like it.

'I did watch it on television but I would have known that your daddy was involved because he would have phoned me to tell me he was OK and if he didn't or he didn't come home then I would know that something wasn't right,' I replied.

William went silent. His face had started to go pale again and I leant down and kissed him and tucked him up on the sofa. I knew that this line of questioning would have exhausted him and it would require a lot of processing before his soul absorbed his situation.

That night I woke up at 3 a.m. and listened to William breathing. I let my eyes adjust to the dark and looked at my beautiful five-year-old son as he slept beside me. No child should have to deal with a situation like this. Suddenly I recognized the shock that the whole experience had had on me. I rushed to the bathroom and threw up. I realized that even if I didn't accept the emotions in a given situation, my body was always quick to acknowledge them.

William itched for the best part of a week. His face and arm were swollen and he had been stung on the side of his nose, which gave him a black eye.

'How many times have I been stung?' he asked as he arranged his war stories in his mind for his friends a few days later.

'You were stung eleven times,' I replied.

PART III
BEING

Chapter Fifteen

'Elizabeth, you need to be the top dog,' Jan explained as we sat on my deck in the back garden one day. William was starting to exercise his rights and we were discussing the issues that are uniquely associated with bringing a child up on your own. 'You have to be in charge, take control, make decisions and feed the group. If at any point one of the pack sees that you're not doing that then they'll try to take charge.'

'I hear what you're saying, but William's only little, he isn't a dog and our pack only has two people in it.' I laughed.

'True,' said Jan, 'but this is William's pack and if he knows that you're in charge and that he's safe, well and looked after, he'll relax. He'll have a safe foundation from which to explore his life.'

I knew that this analogy was right and it helped me to choose what style of parent I wanted to be with William. I had never signed up to be a single parent and if there was anything I was most angry about it was finding myself on my own with a child. The glossy magazines regularly talked about glamorous Hollywood single mothers and I fumed at the image. Single parenting was incredibly hard. I was comforter, chef, DIY person, financier, events organizer, mechanic, banker, teacher, judge and nurse among the myriad roles I played within the house.

I was also continually surrounded by friends with husbands and other children and it was too easy to be jealous of what others had and I lacked. I felt sorry for myself. I wished it was me falling pregnant rather than one of my friends. I missed the supportive arms around me at the end of a hard day.

I placed very high expectations on myself, which didn't help. I felt I had to prove to Simon that I could be a good parent and held myself accountable because everything William did was a demonstration of how successful I was at the job.

Whenever I got frustrated with my situation, though, I remembered Simon standing in the Windows on the World restaurant and I regained my perspective immediately. I stopped and asked myself, 'On the day you die, Elizabeth, what will you look back on most? Your relationship with your child or the time spent wishing your life was different?'

I often sat myself down and took time to look at all the things I was thankful for. I wanted to take everything I'd learnt and the subsequent choices I'd made since Simon's death and apply them to being a mother. I knew I'd developed new values in other areas of my life that could work for me as a single parent. With no one to share the decision-making, it was completely my choice what type of parent I wanted to be. It was liberating on one hand but extremely scary on the other. I didn't know whether I could make it happen on my own. I wanted to be strong and fair and give William unconditional love with boundaries. I also wanted to be fun but know when to draw the line. So I continually reminded myself about the end result – I was bringing William up to be an adult. I had to give him skills he could work with and use for the rest of his life. I started to look at all the values I applied to myself, and then try them out with my son.

By the time William went to school I'd known him longer than I'd known his father. Simon's early death brought home to me how important the role of a parent was and there was nothing more important to me than that job. So I chose to be present in William's life and even though this meant wearing a thousand different hats I felt the privilege of having a child and the experience of being a mother. I decided to enjoy every single ounce of it. I felt very lucky to have my little boy.

When I watched William play, I watched my own heart running around outside of me. I wanted to protect him and keep him safe without projecting my own fear of loss on to him. I learnt that a child couldn't replace the love you have for a partner – it was a different kind of love and should be celebrated and not compared. I love him completely and would do anything to make his life easier, but William has to live his own life and learn his own lessons.

I read a poem called *The Prophet*, by Kahlil Gibran.

Your children are not your children.
They are the sons and daughters of Life's longing for itself.
They come through you but not from you,
And though they are with you they belong not to you.
You may give them your love but not your thoughts ...
You may house their bodies but not their souls ...
You are the bows from which your children as living
   arrows are sent forth.

When Simon was in the World Trade Center I hoped more than anything that he was able to say, 'This is the life I wanted.

185

This was my choice and nobody else's.' That was very important to me. After his death I chose that approach for myself and I wanted it for William too.

He would excel at some things and be less good at others but he needed the space to find that out for himself. He needed to work out who William was. I could help him develop the ability to choose who he was going to be but I shouldn't judge him or expect anything in return.

One evening he came home from school and explained that one of his friends kept asking him to do something he didn't want to do.

'William, can I ask you if you've been born to live William Turner's life or your friend's life?' I put to him.

William looked at me with his piercing brown eyes as he thought about this.

'I've been born to have William's life, of course,' he replied.

'Then it doesn't matter whether a friend really wants you to do something – you have to listen to what's inside William and see what it's telling you. Only you know what you want to do,' I explained carefully.

I encouraged him to cook, load the dishwasher, wash the car and clean up after himself. I taught him how to let out his anger or sadness and then how to calm himself down afterwards. I showed him that he could shout as loud as he wanted in the park or by the sea but he had to talk quietly in shops and at the queue in Tesco. I showed him how to save his pocket money and how to blow birthday money in one go for enjoyment.

When parents say they want their child to be free to be themselves it can imply there are no rules and regulations. I had to work out how to apply boundaries too. A friend told me that when I first explained how I wanted to approach bringing up William, she thought he would be a spoilt child, but she had watched me work very hard to achieve the delicate balance between a framework of rules to live by and William's right to explore his own identity. I operated a 'cause and effect' policy in the house, which demonstrated that choices came with consequences. I tried to show William that he could do anything he wanted but if he chose X then Y would happen. It showed him that not only could he choose what to do but he could choose the outcome he wanted as well. On the day he drew all over the hallway wall, William found himself with a cloth cleaning all the pen marks off by himself. He has never done it since.

I regularly used the phrase, 'Because I love you, William, I am going to let you learn through your mistakes . . .' to remind myself that doing things for William or trying to make it right for him prevented him learning for himself and was not ultimately in his best interests. So William knew that if he was rude I wouldn't talk to him, if he hit a friend they wouldn't play with him, if he ate too much he would feel sick and if he teased the cats or the dog he could get scratched and bitten. It was hard but I knew that William would have a toolbox for his adult life which would help him create a future he wanted, having considered all the implications first.

William sometimes asked if I loved him when he'd been told off and I comforted him by saying, 'I love you always, even if I might not like a choice you made.'

Early one morning William climbed into bed with me. 'Did Daddy like me?' he asked quietly.

William always picked the most inopportune moments to ask me these questions. It was about 6 a.m. and I was still half-asleep so somewhere in the depths of my dreams I had to rally my brain and provide a healthy answer.

Even in my drowsy state I could work out where William's thoughts were coming from.

'Just because Daddy died doesn't mean he didn't like you. From the day he knew I was pregnant he loved you and still does love you, completely,' I reassured him.

I needed to help William understand the concept of love. He had a very real example of someone who loved him leaving him.

'There are times when people you love have to go away. Sometimes that's their choice and sometimes it's not. It wasn't your daddy's choice to die, but he still loves you regardless,' I explained.

I made a point of showing him how lucky he was to have so many people who loved him in his life and we regularly counted the people in his family. We also included the people who were friends and whose support I'd come to appreciate so much. William might not have a father or siblings but we created an extended family that we cared for and who loved us too. Simon's father left when he was very young and remarried so William has a half-aunty, Daniela, who is only twenty-two, and she has formed a wonderful bond with him. After she had been staying with us for a couple of days and then gone home, William looked at me and said, 'I love being with Daniela. It's like spending time with my dad.' He instinctively recognizes that she is the closest he'll get to Simon.

I'd made sure that there was lots of love in William's world, which was easy to arrange. We often talked about how we loved each other even when we were grumpy, tired or sad, and when he sometimes told me that he was cross and didn't love me any more I simply replied, 'William, it doesn't matter because I love you anyway, all the time. I love you regardless.'

This platform of unconditional love gave him security but I knew I had to provide discipline too and show him that his life was his own responsibility.

There were other times when I found William extremely challenging. I realized that despite all my studies and work experience with everyone from students to board directors this small boy could test me to the limit. On one particular day when I was struggling with him and taking the opportunity to voice my frustrations, Jan gave me some perspective on the situation.

'Don't forget, Elizabeth, that William is a product of both you and Simon.'

I let my mind wander through this statement with all its implications.

'Oh no,' I groaned. 'Let's hope he has all the good bits of Simon and me otherwise he'll be wilful, grumpy, determined and persistent!'

So what has William provided me with? Laughter, joy, learning, growth and constant change. He has kept my heart open and probably opened it wider. He has shown me how to love again and he has given me a reason to accept only the exceptional in my life. He is a daily reminder to make my life the best it can be, with no excuses. This 'best' doesn't mean success and achievement any more – it means balance and time and joy. I have learnt to plan my life in pencil with William. I make plans, create goals and provide security for the future but I can always rub them out and change my mind. He reminds me to live in the now and not to take myself too seriously.

William also helped me stop trying to achieve perfection and to enjoy what I learnt from bringing up a child. He has been my greatest teacher. I felt I had a huge responsibility to be a good parent to William. I had to get it right and prove that I could bring up our son in a way that would make Simon proud of me. William, of course, demonstrated regularly that he wasn't a social experiment but a little boy making his way in the world, and all the plans I had were good in theory but often weak in practice. One afternoon after school William and I were sitting in the kitchen together having tea. William gave Archie some of the sausages off his plate and I told him he had to stop. I then launched into a long explanation of why.

'William, do you know why I'm asking you to stop?' I continued without waiting for an answer. 'Archie shouldn't be given food from the table as it encourages him to beg and to be a nuisance while we're eating. It's the wrong food for him and we're not allowed to be near Archie when he eats his food. Also, if Archie sees us giving him food from the table then he may take it to another level and start taking food from the table as well.' I stopped to take a breath.

'Do you understand what I'm saying?' I asked William. There was no reply.

'William, did you hear what I said?' I repeated.

William lifted his head, looked at me and very innocently explained, 'Mummy, I only heard some of what you said. You use so many words that I can't hear all of them.'

I looked at William as he continued eating, and laughed. I

190

learnt to keep all my instructions and explanations very short from then on.

I think that now I also have more appreciation of the fact that William is a boy. I enjoy it and have had to learn a lot, and it has challenged me more than a girl might have done. There are so many things he does that are like Simon and so many things I enjoy watching and learning.

It's probably one other aspect of him being a boy, together with the gap that exists in his family world, that's given William a new goal.

'Have you found me a new daddy?' William asked me nonchalantly one day.

I laughed. If only it were that simple! It wasn't like it had been before when I was single. Then, people asked what I did for a living and I could answer in one sentence with no subclauses. Now I found it hard to tell people what I did and who I was. But I also knew I was reaching a place where I could seriously think about life with a partner again and the connection that brought. It wasn't until I thought about dating, though, that I realized there were aspects of Simon's death I hadn't truly understood. I'd assumed that my life with Simon had set a template, and that my ability to love him, get married and have a child with him meant that I would be able to find that joy again.

What I hadn't realized was how much confidence I'd lost. I wasn't sure whether this was because of becoming a parent or a widow. I felt battered, exhausted by the enormity of the task, out of touch and not at my best as a woman. Some of my dating experiences did nothing to alleviate these fears. One date questioned why I was a widow at such a young age and, before I could begin to explain, offered the suggestion that my husband had committed suicide. One man told me how his dog slept with him at night, and another gleefully explained that the charming, off-the-beaten-track restaurant he'd brought me to was where prostitutes came to grab something to eat after their shift. I felt I was living in a different universe most of the time, but for some reason thought it was good to be putting myself out there and showing the world that I had moved on and was capable of having a new relationship.

'I've found someone for you, Mummy,' said William one day.

'Oh, who's that?' I asked tentatively.

'Well, someone who doesn't have a home and they can come and live with us,' he declared matter-of-factly.

'Who would that be?'

'The people in Muswell Hill who sell the magazines outside the shops,' he said.

'The homeless people who sell the *Big Issue* magazine?'

'Yes, that's it! Kate [who used to look after William a couple of days a week] told me about them,' he said triumphantly, believing that the whole situation was sorted.

'That's a very nice thought, William, but a new daddy has to be someone Mummy loves and someone I want to spend the rest of my life with. It isn't a case of just picking out someone who's available, but finding someone you want to be with,' I declared.

I knew that all my family and friends would be delighted if I met someone else and even I knew it was fine to have a relationship again and that Simon would be pleased for me. But I didn't want people to think that just finding someone to replace Simon would automatically create a happily-ever-after solution. I'd had to walk through my grief and live my life by a new philosophy in order to find peace and it was because I'd achieved this peace that I was now in a position to consider meeting someone and enjoying a future with them. I tried to explain this as best I could to my small son.

'I could meet a lot of people and still not find someone to be a new daddy. I'm looking for someone I can love and who will love me back, and you too. That's very important. We don't want any old daddy, do we?' I was pleased with my answer.

'Yes we do. How about my headmaster at school?' he volunteered.

'I think you'll find that he's married with a new baby.'

'What about him?' William suggested, pointing at the plumber who was kindly sorting out a leak in the kitchen.

'I think it would be best if you leave the choosing of a new daddy to me,' I concluded. 'Trust me that I'll find a new daddy who'll want to be part of our family, if he's out there!'

I walked around Highgate Woods with Archie and reviewed my life. William did have a point. Where was I with all of this? What did I want to do with myself now that he was at school?

I had looked after William to the point that he was asking me for a new daddy but most of all I had looked after myself. I was no longer trying to convince the outside world that my life was fulfilled. I had discovered my own inner peace and chosen to create something new. I genuinely felt whole and at peace. I was truly being me.

However, I still had to decide what I wanted my future to look like, whether it was going to involve a partner or not. How did I want to use everything I'd learnt on my journey, and how was I going to create a situation where my work and life were a seamless continuation of who I was? I had been given a second chance after Simon's death and this was the one thing I was never going to squander.

I knew that I wanted to create my life around William. He was already without one parent and I didn't want him to be without two. I also knew that I wanted to leave a footprint behind that reflected Simon's life and death and to help others who had experienced traumatic events in their life. I needed a career that had meaning. I had a deep desire to make a difference in the world and to show William that the choices I'd made were worth it to do something that created positive change. I didn't know how to achieve this but I knew my intent was strong and clear. I was trying not to control my route but to allow my life to flow and to see what was presented to me. This was hard and I could see that I'd gone down a few blind alleys. I was still learning to trust that if I paid attention to the signs along the path I would find the right role for me.

In the year after Simon died I set up a charity called 'Simon & US' which provided a holistic approach to grief and loss. It was the first charity in the UK authorized by the Charity Commission to provide Reiki healing as a therapy. We had raised a lot of money but somewhere deep inside I knew it wasn't quite what I was looking for. It wasn't that I was lacking in support as there was a strong and dedicated team of people who wanted to work with it and move it forward. But the charity framework didn't feel right in relation to my own values and beliefs post 11 September. I liked freedom and creativity and there were too many rules and regulations within the charity structure. I also knew that I wanted to work for myself and not be part of a corporate organization.

With this in mind and knowing that my focus at the moment had to be William, I made the difficult decision to close the charity. I had to be true to myself. If I did what was right for me, then the bigger picture would work itself out to make it right for everyone else too. The charity had reached a dead end and it was OK to back up and try another path.

I knew I couldn't go back to my HR job. It would have been wrong for all of us. 11 September had happened, my previous life had gone and I had been given a blank canvas to try something new. I felt deeply that it would be insulting to Simon if I said to his son, after he'd died in this enormous event, 'This is how your daddy died, it was awful and then I went back to work and carried on as normal.'

I had a much greater spiritual understanding of my situation now. I really felt that everything happened for a reason and that I could create the life I wanted. So I decided to keep searching and eliminate what I didn't want – the same approach that had helped me through my grief.

There were aspects of my HR career that I still enjoyed and I realized that coaching was something I didn't want to leave behind. On one of Simon's business trips he'd flown from New York to California. It was unusual for him to strike up conversations on a plane, preferring instead to sleep or catch up on reading. But on this occasion, the man sitting next to him introduced himself as David Woods and they got talking. David ran his own coaching company and training programme.

'That's interesting,' said Simon. 'My wife is interested in doing some coaching.'

'Well, here's my card,' replied David. 'She can have a look at my website and give me a call if she wants to take it further.'

After Simon died, I remembered the card. I had been interested in life coaching but before Simon's death I didn't believe I had any significant life experience to substantiate such a career choice. I emailed David and asked whether he remembered Simon and the conversation. He did, and after looking at his website I enrolled with the International Coaching Academy. The course was an internet-based programme which was affiliated with the International Coaching Federation. I chose to do my courses through home learning, which worked around William's life. I had teleclasses linked up to the lecturers, I downloaded the course materials and I submitted my work online. For my own development I had to work regularly with clients to build up my coaching hours. I loved the thought that Simon was still helping – finding me a course that would develop my skills while still allowing me to be with our son.

I had also decided to qualify as a Reiki Master/Trainer. It was Reiki that had ultimately provided me with the quietness I so desperately searched for in the immediate aftermath of 11 September. I wanted to be able to share its peace with others so I completed my Reiki training from Attunement 1 and 2 to Master and Trainer and registered with the UK Reiki Federation. I took each course and in between I set up a couch in my back room and practised my new skills on friends and family, building up my hours in both Reiki and coaching.

Initially I worked part time so as to balance my time with William against time spent developing my career and studying. I needed to see how this new life worked as a representation of who I really was. My coaching business was successful and I enjoyed it but when the opportunity came up to work with a group of like-minded individuals I jumped at it. I hadn't realized I wanted to work with other people, but I'd been letting life flow and watching for changes and new directions, and when it appeared I chose this new path.

With Jan and another colleague, Kevin, I set up a limited company – ulife ltd (www.ulife.co.uk) – providing life-coaching, Reiki and NLP (Neuro-Linguistic Programming) development workshops and training courses. We have a range of clients from private individuals to groups, charities and corporate organizations, and we focus on all areas of life change. My experience has taught me that loss is not just about bereavement. For some it could be the breakdown of a marriage, a child who is ill or the loss of a job, but all of these share the loss of normality, and each experience is as life-changing to the individual as 11 September was to me.

Our company helps clients to take responsibility for their life by responding to their change, rather than simply changing to something else. It's not about what has happened to you but how you deal with it that matters and ulife works to show people how to empower themselves to deal with all that life has to offer. We show them how to manage their life, discover the tools that work for them, handle anything that happens and develop their own emotional guidance system.

We have worked with clients in many areas – breast cancer, bereavement, divorce, trauma, redundancy and corporate change. It is very important that our clients understand that we know what it's like to deal with change. They can take comfort from the fact that we're not just reading from a book but know from our own experience what it's like to deal with life-changing events.

The set-up works for me too. I am challenged, responsible

for my own outcomes and able to manage my time with William and to leave positive change behind me. My work is a complete reflection of who I am.

So all aspects of my life were in a good place – even Archie the dog. But what about William's new daddy?

I knew that the relationship I'd had with Simon was a special part of my life, I knew because of it how wonderful a relationship can be and I wanted to have that again. I will always love Simon and he will always be a big part of my life but I was ready to open myself up to the prospect of a new relationship. I had thought I needed to find closure after Simon's death but instead I discovered that I could take Simon's love with me as part of who I am now. I know now I can survive any amount of change, but more importantly I can grow through it and be greater because of it.

My way of saying how much I love Simon is to live the whole of life. It is because of how important he was to me that I choose to make my life meaningful. If it were me that had died, I would want him to live the richest, fullest, most amazing life, particularly if he had my son with him.

Because I was a different person now, I wasn't looking for another Simon. The next relationship would be based on the new values and beliefs I lived by. But it had to match the quality of my relationship with Simon or be richer than what we'd shared before he died. I couldn't accept less than that, either for me or for William.

On 11 September 2008 at the launch of ulife ltd, someone I'd met many years earlier came to support the new business. I hadn't seen him for a long time and when he walked into the event and we hugged, I knew I'd met someone very special.

I am walking again. I have absorbed the whole experience of 11 September and I am being who I want to be after everything I've learnt. I am a parent, a partner, a sister, a daughter, a Reiki trainer, a coach, a director, a colleague, a friend and a mum. I love all of it and I have chosen all of it. I am thankful for every one of them.

Chapter Sixteen

'Before booking any old thing have you really asked your-self where you want to celebrate and with whom?' Catherine volunteered after I read out a very long list of party venues across London.

She was right. My fortieth birthday felt important on so many levels. It wasn't just about marking an age, it was an opportunity to celebrate a life of experience and all the relationships and situations that had helped me grow into my soul. I wanted to say thank you to everyone who'd helped me get here and for all I'd learnt in the process. My thirties had all been about Simon, William and 11 September and I wanted to pack up my new knowledge and take it into the next part of my life.

The celebrations should reflect all the things I held dear in my life, and when I thought about that I knew the answer to my dilemma. I would hold a party at home, the place that had kept me and William safe. I would have a children's party in the afternoon to celebrate with all the friends who'd helped me as a single parent and to enjoy the special part that William had played. Then I'd have an adults' party in the evening to say thank you to everyone who mattered to me and to recognize who I was now. I wasn't only a mum or a widow from

11 September. My journey since Simon's death had shown me so much more of who I was and I wanted to celebrate that too.

I wasn't an entirely different person. I had the same sense of humour and still enjoyed the same things – walking the dog, dinner with friends, time with my family. But the philosophy I lived my life by had changed and I could see that I hadn't dealt only with the grief of Simon's loss. Every time I came up against something difficult I returned to the values that had worked for me after 11 September. And when I did, they helped me to navigate through the turbulence.

On 11 September 2001 everything I had ever believed in was completely destroyed. I stood and faced death – my own as well as Simon's – square in the face and found that it was the greatest teacher I had ever met.

Death is our eternal companion.
It is always to our left, at an arm's length.
It has always been watching you.
It always will until the day it taps you.

The thing to do when you're impatient is . . . to turn to
    your left and ask advice from your death.
An immense amount of pettiness is dropped if your death
    makes a gesture to you,
or if you catch a glimpse of it,
or if you just catch the feeling that your companion is there
    watching you.

(Carlos Castaneda)

I'd had a choice then. I could take my own life or stay and face the most difficult journey ever. Somewhere deep in the darkest place in my soul, seeing that I had this choice shone a light. The universe showed me the truth about life, love, why we're here and what our purpose is, and in that light I saw that my journey was my responsibility and only I could choose what happened next or even how it would end.

So many people helped me, all wanting to hold me up and take some of the pain so that I could live again. Their support was immeasurable. But I realized I had to walk this path on my own. Only I could face it if I was to come out on the other side.

This was the turning point. I realized that all the choices in my life were my responsibility and that my emotions were there to guide me. Reiki and life coaching helped me to feel the potential in my emotions and to interpret them so I always grew through my pain rather than being destroyed by it. I learnt to listen to my heart, not my head, so that I could truly feel and understand my experience and discover a more enriched life. This understanding helped me to see something else.

My life before 11 September was typical of modern-day society. I was busy, everything moved very fast and I rarely sat down and took time to reflect. I didn't notice what I was really being. It took something as huge as Simon's death to make me stop and look around. In that moment I had to look at my life's values and determine what was important to me in the new landscape and what was not.

In this process I discovered the deep secret of humanity, which is that we already have everything within us to support ourselves throughout our lives. It seems that it takes the force of incomparable life-changing circumstances to open up the knowledge that sits within us. All the tools I ever needed to help me work my way through Simon's death were inside me. I didn't know how to access them and I didn't know how to use them but once I was shown, using Reiki and life coaching, I was able to put them into practice and they guided me through the wreckage.

I could see that this knowledge within me was like the list of beliefs at the Rockefeller Center in New York. I wanted them as the new framework for my life, and for them to reflect the choices I made in my relationships and my work. I realized that within my belief system there were eleven choices, and for the first time I wrote them down:

Responsibility – to know that your life belongs to you and that every experience, whether good or bad, is your own responsibility and creates choice.

Perspective – to view every situation with the bigger picture in mind. The world and life look very different from above.

Signs – to remember that the world moves in mysterious ways and the signs are there to point you in the direction that works for your highest purpose.

Intuition – to use your intuition to guide you. It is your individual guide for life and no one else's.

Emotion – to feel your emotion and to look for understanding in the messages that are held within it.

Trust – to trust your inner guide and the bigger picture of life even when it looks impossible.

Intention – to know that everything works if the intent behind it comes straight from your heart.

Respect – to respect yourself and everything you believe and to respect others' choices on their journeys too. It is not your place to judge someone else's path.

Truth – to be truthful to yourself and others at all times even when it hurts.

Love – to love yourself and everyone else unconditionally.

Forgiveness – to forgive from the heart is to know that you are here to learn and that the most challenging experiences and relationships will always be your greatest teachers.

Seeing the choices in black and white was like having a light bulb switched on. They allowed me to stay anchored in the storm, they helped me find a meaning in Simon's death and they helped me interpret the events as my teachers rather than my persecutors. I now had a tangible framework that I could use for everything in my life. Without them I might have looked to the outside world as though I were living. I would still be out with friends, going on holiday and even dating again but I know I would not have been whole and definitely not at peace in my heart. It was because of the choices that the 'peace' quote always resonated with me.

Peace. It does not mean to be in a place where there is no noise, trouble or hard work. It means to be in the midst of those things and still be calm in your heart.

I know that I have grown lifetimes since Simon's death and that this knowledge is precious. I am fully present in my life and have the freedom to be truly who I am and to live the life I want to live. I don't feel the need to compare myself or my life to others, or to wish I had other things that friends had. The choices have become the principles by which I live my life.

So that's the end of my story – or is it? There is a 'happily ever after' ending like all good fairy tales but not because everything in my life is perfect and sorted. The happy ending is because through a painful journey of self-discovery I have learnt that the hardest things in life can hide the most precious secrets.

As I stand on the other side of the mountain and take in the new horizon I am full of gratitude for the immense journey I have been on. It is a privilege to have walked the path from 11 September 2001 and to know that the love of Simon, the love for William and the eleven choices have given me the opportunity to create a new life that is richer, deeper, more colourful and more at peace than ever before.

Every day is a special gift full of wondrous moments, generous and loving people and great peace and joy. Everything is a learning opportunity to help me grow and continually evolve to reach my full potential. Everything I choose to create I am thankful for. I treasure every relationship, and tell people how important they are to me. I have learnt how to live my life for myself and now have the opportunity to help others create the framework for their own life.

I choose the path I have taken because I loved Simon from my soul and anything less would have been an insult to what we had together. Simon gave me the two most precious gifts when he died – the will to understand his death in relation to my life and the bigger picture, and William. He was an exceptional man and he lived an exceptional life and he gave me the opportunity to lead an exceptional life too. I know I have faced all the lessons from 11 September 2001 and that Simon would be proud. I know William will be proud, but most of all I am proud of myself.

On the last page of the journal I kept after Simon died I have written a goodbye that came from my heart. I can say goodbye to our relationship knowing that the love and connection we had will always be with me and that I have absorbed everything our relationship was meant to be.

I wrote:

To my darling Simon
I love you and always will
You gave me the greatest gifts ever
You gave me your life so I could grow and develop and you
*   gave me William*
The greatest love of all
You have a piece of my heart always
A piece of me died with you
But it is now time to move forward
We will meet again
I promise to fulfil my destiny
Keep the champagne cold
Love you forever
Goodbye, All my love Elizabeth/Wifey

So this is where I am now.

Afterword, 2011

The question I have been asked most frequently since writing this book is what I think about the world after 11 September 2001.

This morning, as I lay wrapped in my duvet waiting for the house to wake up, the radio clicked on. I lay there quietly listening to the news as John Humphrys analysed the day's events around the world and I heard the words '9/11' float out into the room. That phrase seems to be a part of the English language now. Even if I wanted to stop thinking about what happened that day, I can't. Ten years on we are still talking about it, still witnessing the ripple effects and we are all still deeply involved in choosing how we want our world to be in the aftermath.

How has the world changed in the past ten years? How have I changed? What lessons have any of us learnt in that time? Do we act differently towards each other because all those people died on a beautiful autumn day in 2001? Are we kinder to people that we don't know? Are we less judgemental of things that we don't understand? Are we teaching our children to respond to the world differently? Are any of us choosing a different path to the one we were shown ten years ago? In fact, how would I answer any of these questions myself?

I recently had a conversation with William after school one evening.

'We're doing black history at school at the moment, Mum,' he told me.

'What will that cover?' I asked him. I always want to hear about the subjects that William and his class mates are being introduced to; they seem much more interesting than when I was at school.

'Well, we are going to look at Martin Luther King, Nelson Mandela and Barak Obama, I think' he remembered.

'Do you know why any of these people are important in the history of the world?' I questioned.

'We've only started to look at Barak Obama and that's because he was the first black President in the United States' he explained.

'That's right' I replied.

'Why is that such a big deal?' He continued. 'I don't get why skin colour is such a big deal?'

In William's class there are children with different skin colours, religions, and cultural backgrounds so he thinks it is completely normal to live like that and to just play together.

'In history, William, there have been many times when people thought they were better than others because they had a different coloured skin, followed a particular religion or came from a certain place. They believed there was only one way to live and anything else was wrong.'

'That's mad!' William replied and continued eating his supper.

I'm proud that he thinks that. We may all live in different places in this world, look different and believe different things but at the end of the day we are all human beings. When Simon stood on the 106th floor of the World Trade Centre and faced his death with all the other people trapped with him, everything else was stripped away. They were just human beings thinking about their loved ones. Why can't we see this and find ways to live together?

Over the last ten years there have been the 7 July bombings, the 2004 Tsunami, Bali bombings, the earthquakes in Haiti, Christchurch and Japan and countless other personal disasters that have not made the news. So many traumatic things have happened to other people. There are many families being told their loved ones won't be returning from army duties in Afghanistan and Iraq and there are many civilians caught up in global conflicts. One talk I gave for a Macmillan Cancer Research fundraiser proved to be one of the most challenging as I realised my audience was made up entirely of people who had lived through World War II.

I often hear, 'But your experience is so much bigger than mine' and yet I'm sure that if Simon had been hit by a bus, my grief would have been no easier to face. Through all the different clients I have worked with and people I meet when I do talks I can see that everyone has their own 11 September to face in their life. It doesn't matter how big or small it looks to anyone else, we all have to face our own mountain at some point.

As I look at my experiences of the last ten years I realise I don't need to comment on the world stage post 9/11 because it is still being commented on and it will be for many more years to come. 11 September 2001 has become a metaphor for change both for the world and for individuals.

Since the book was published I have received many letters and emails from people it has affected, thanking me for sharing my journey and helping them on theirs. I am immeasurably touched by all the people who took the time to tell me that what I did helped – and is still helping them – when they found themselves in dark places. It's enough that my story has achieved that.

For me, personally, one email I was sent after the book had been published, says it all:

Dear Elizabeth

I stumbled across your book when a friend I work with was reading it. I borrowed it over the weekend and now on Monday morning I'm writing to you having finished it last night.

I wanted to thank you for sharing your story. I lost my brother when I was 5 years old (he was 15). I am now 34 and am only just beginning to realise what a profound impact his death has had on my family. Your story really resonated with me. I think it came at just the right time. I know I will take lessons from it and I will use them to make positive choices and changes in my life. All when the timing is right.

Thank you so much.

Kindest regards

At the beginning of the book I wrote about what I had wanted to do after Simon died. Achieving those things was not simply a box-ticking exercise on the road to getting my life together. Ten years on, I can look back and I am amazed. What I have learnt over the last ten years is that in every storm there is always the opportunity to choose how you want to react; there is always a new landscape to embrace; and there is always the chance to learn new things and to break the limitations that only we put on ourselves.

When I met Dave shortly after my 40th birthday, I knew I'd found someone like Simon, someone I could let go with and spend my life with. And it frightened me.

'Do you think he's going to die on you, then?' my sister Catherine asked directly.

'When you put it like that, I know it sounds ridiculous! But, when Simon died the pain of the grief was directly proportionate to the depth of my love for him. The more you love the more you feel the grief. I don't think I want to go there again.'

'Then you're not living,' Catherine pointed out. 'And no one could accuse you of rushing into it, could they?!'

I have a framed quote hanging at the top of my stairs.

For a long time it seemed to me that life was about to begin, real life.

But, there was always some obstacle in the way, something to be gotten through first,

Some unfinished business, time still to be served or a debt to be paid. Then life would begin.

At last it dawned on me that there is no way to happiness. Happiness is the way.

Happiness is a journey, not a destination.

So work like you don't need the money, Love like you have never been hurt, and Dance like no one's watching.'

D'Souza.

*   *   *

'We were making Father's Day cards today at school,' William explained on the walk home one evening. Archie was doing his usual hoovering up of every take-away he could find and we were trying to negotiate the busy junction at the end of the road from William's school. In the past William had made cards for Granddad and Henry his godfather too. This year felt different though, as Dave and I were now living together and Dave's daughter, Emily, was moving in with us whilst she did an internship in London for the year. His son, Tom, was a regular visitor too. I loved what we all had together and I knew that William loved his new extended family. But whatever I might wish for in the relationship between William and Dave it wasn't something that I could make happen.

'That sounds like a fun afternoon,' I replied cautiously.

'I made mine for Dave. Do you think he'll like it?' William asked.

My eyes pricked with emotion as I carried on yanking Archie away from the cold chips in front of his nose.

'William, I know he will absolutely love it.' I couldn't help smiling to myself.

So, on Father's Day a triumphant boy gave Dave the card he had made.

'I love it mate!' William and Dave did the customary high five when they mutually agreed on something. What Dave did next was completely unexpected.

'Have you made your Dad a card this year too?' he asked.

'No, I haven't.' William replied.

'Would you like to make one for him? Would you like me to help you make one?' Dave suggested. William's face erupted into a huge beaming smile.

'I'd love that!' he exclaimed.

By the end of the day, we had enjoyed a large family roast with Tom and Emily joining us to spend Father's Day with their dad. Afterwards, we all went outside and stood around the barbecue, and in the style of the Tibetan monks we burnt the card that Dave and William had made and sent it to Simon.

Acknowledgements

I have thanked everyone individually and many times over the last few years but I can never say it enough . . .

Mum and Dad – you gave me everything parents could give their child so that I could face the ultimate test in my life. Thank you for loving me so much that you gave me the skills an adult needs to face life with courage. You are both greatly loved by me and William.

Deborah, Mark, Catherine and Ron – you stood right next to me at my darkest time. I can never thank you enough for being there but I can tell you how much I love you.

Andrew, Jo, Kate, Tom, Harry, Matthew, James, Charlie and Pippy – for letting them all be with me and for being part of the privilege that I call my family.

Tom and Emily – for making William and me so welcome and for being the brother and sister that William always hoped for. I love sharing our life together.

Jane and Henry – you were with me when William was born and you and your family have been with us both ever since. I love what we share.

Jan – you were the trigger that opened my eyes in the dark. You showed me that my journey and my life belonged to me and everything I needed was within me. Because of your support I was able to stand up and walk on my own again.

Pete – for your friendship with me through everything. I know Simon was proud that you were his friend and his best man.

Keith – for making such a difficult trip to NYC on my behalf. I will always be grateful for your love and support at that time.

Celine – for sharing the friendship you had with Simon with me. I have valued it through everything and always will.

Jill – you always listened and took time to understand but the best part has been sharing my spiritual journey with you.

Amanda – it was as if you were handpicked for me and my family and were an extension of us all. You held my hand through everything with incredible sensitivity.

Nick and James – for caring about William so much after your own experience and sharing the start of his life.

Helen – for a fine array of pyjamas, for A & E runs, illness checks and for supporting me unquestioningly every single time I asked for help.

Caroline – for all your book support since day one and a deep, enduring friendship through many challenges.

Mick Gillard – for giving me the precious memories of William's birth when I thought that would never be possible.

BO – for being everything you are and for helping all of us. You are a very special man.

The Portland team, in particular Breda and Terese – for looking after me so incredibly that William's birth was something I was able to stop worrying about.

The HAC, in particular Steve Ashley, Johnny Longbottom and David Reindorp – for showing me the HAC that Simon had always told me about and loved.

The Marathon team – for so much fun in Boston when it was missing from my life, and for the incredible feat I can tell William about.

Andy Ranson – for a great friendship out of the marathon and to show that you weren't on the editing floor.

The AHAC – for all your support on the marathon trip and in particular Joe and Marilyn Benoit, who William and I are proud to call his American grandparents.

Risk Waters – to everyone who helped me even when I wasn't aware of it. I knew there was a lot of careful thought that went into so many things at a difficult time for all of us.

Peter Meier, Jane Jordan and everyone at Channel 4 – for your care and thoughtfulness as employers which were above and beyond the call of duty. It made a huge difference in my life.

Kevin – we met as fellow coaches and our journey took us to a great friendship.

Daniela – you have been a joy to meet in my life because of Simon. William and I can't believe how lucky we are to have you as part of our family too.

Radi – I would definitely drop all the balls if you weren't part of our lives. Thank you for everything you do for us.

Heather – for all your coaching and guidance that kept me and my book deadlines completely on track.

My girl friends – for endless talks of support, for helping with William, for believing in me and still being there when I couldn't juggle all the balls: Alice, Anette, Anya, Debs, Gabby,

Jenny, Jo, Kate H, Ranjana, Sara, Sarah P., Sarah S., Sharon, Sue A.

All my friends on the twenty-four-hour rota – for your presence and immense support even if I never appreciated any of your food!

All my friends and neighbours, in particular Andy and Tony G., who helped me with everything from phoning to say they would wait till I was ready to socialize, to mending broken things in the house, financial help and loving support, and for keeping in regular contact.

All the people whose names I don't know, from the guardian angel nurse to those who quietly helped me behind the scenes even when I wasn't aware of it.

All the Family Liaison Officers I had the pleasure to know – for doing such sensitive work in such a professional yet compassionate way.

Peta – for weaving your magic and being the best translator. I have loved our edit days.

Araminta – for seeing in my writing what I couldn't see and for recognizing that I needed to write my book for William.

Kerri and everyone at Simon & Schuster – for understanding my story's message from the first day and making it real.

Jackie Llewellyn-Bowen – thank you for all your help but particularly for the introduction to Araminta.

The Red Cross and everyone who donated – for your support when I needed it most. You helped a new mother feel very safe and I will never forget that.

To everyone I interviewed – I really appreciate the time and emotion you gave me, and that you were prepared to revisit a difficult time. I couldn't put everything in but it was an important opportunity for me to talk and share with some very special people and I want to thank you for helping me create this book for William.

All my clients – I feel very privileged that you have shared some of your journey with me and you have all given me so much inspiration.

Everyone who emailed me – I am deeply touched when you take the time to personally thank me for writing the book. I never cease to be amazed by the courage of others.

Dave – I had always hoped that after the journey I had been on, the universe would present a new partner for me who reflected everything I had seen and learnt. I feel very privileged that you have chosen to walk with me and that our journey will be made together for the rest of our lives. I love you, more than.

William – you gave me the reason to stay and I hope you will understand that I did the best I could with what I had and I did it all because I love you. Your daddy would be very proud of the boy that you are. I know I am.

Simon – for your love, our son and my precious memories. I will love you forever and I hope you are proud of where we are now.